the power of
BLESSING

the power of
BLESSING

KERRY KIRKWOOD

DESTINY IMAGE® PUBLISHERS, INC.

P.O. Box 310, Shippensburg, PA 17257-0310

"Speaking to the Purposes of God for This Generation and for the Generations to Come."

This book and all other Destiny Image, Revival Press, MercyPlace, Fresh Bread, Destiny Image Fiction, and Treasure House books are available at Christian bookstores and distributors worldwide.

For a U.S. bookstore nearest you, call 1-800-722-6774.

For more information on foreign distributors, call 717-532-3040.

Reach us on the Internet: www.destinyimage.com.

Trade Paper ISBN 13: 978-0-7684-3232-9
Hardcover ISBN 13: 978-0-7684-3418-7
Large Print ISBN 13: 978-0-7684-3419-4
Ebook ISBN 13: 978-0-7684-9064-0

For Worldwide Distribution, Printed in the U.S.A.

1 2 3 4 5 6 7 8 9 10 11 / 13 12 11 10

ACKNOWLEDGMENTS

L ittle did I know that what started out as a random Sunday morning sermon would become a life message. This life message we now call *The Power of Blessing* has been forged not only in my own life, but in the lives of countless churches around the world. The question began very subtly. More people than I could count would ask, "Do you have this in book form?" I would dismiss the idea with a half laugh, thinking there was no way I could write a book.

The reality of this book has been largely due to the encouragement of my life partner and wife, Diane, who has practiced the life of blessing and has reminded me to do the same. We are grateful for our four children—Casey, Kevin, Kristen, and Kara—for being the testing-ground for this experiment of declaring blessing. They all have experienced the favor of God because of it.

I am thankful for well-timed friends like Ron Simpkins, whose gentle pressure led me to take the first steps to bring this message to a larger platform. It was through Ron that I was introduced to Loua Clair, who would take unedited teaching CDs and put this message on paper with great patience and painstaking effort. Thanks, Loua, for being the catalyst to this book and making this all come together. Your creative skills will be enjoyed by many for years to come.

Along my path of discovery is the congregation of Trinity Fellowship Church in Tyler, Texas, which I have had the pleasure of serving for 22 years. It was your hunger and positive response that caused me to continue pursuing the power that was locked up in blessing. You pulled depths out of me that needed to be discovered.

I owe a great deal to the staff pastors of Trinity Fellowship. This dedicated team of pastors—Duane Hett, Jim Hahn, Harold Vincent, and Leah Brown—has gone beyond just doing their job. They have given me the freedom to go beyond the mundane.

It is with great fondness and joy that I have the privilege of serving with Pastor Olen Griffing, who has been instrumental in developing a prophetic heart of worship in me. His integrity has been a rock for me to test my own heart as I walked out these principles. His leadership as an apostle over the Antioch Oasis Network of Churches has been invaluable. To Dick and Sue Bontke, thank you for the consistent nudge to take the message of blessing to the nations. Your friendship has been refreshing to Diane and me. Thank you to all the Antioch Oasis pastors; I have enjoyed sharing the Power of Blessing in your congregations. You have been a source of encouragement to finish and finish well. May we have many more years together exploring the depths of our God together.

To my good friend Cleddie Keith, who has been a rich source of affirmation to me. Thanks, Cleddie, for your encouragement to go beyond the surface and dive into the depths of the Spirit.

Endorsements

As an avid reader I enjoy reading books. Although my level of enjoyment varies, I always get something of value from each book. Seldom do I read a book I can hardly put down... *The Power of Blessing* is one of those. This is a "have to read" book for believers and unbelievers alike if they have any desire to live a life full of joy.

Olen Griffing
Senior Pastor, Shady Grove Church
Grand Prairie, Texas

There will, no doubt, be some who pick up this book, read the cover, and say, "I am familiar with this teaching; it is more of the same." That is far from the truth. The first time I heard Kerry Kirkwood teach I realized he was a man with whom God had entrusted transforming truth. I begged him to get this into print for the benefit of families and those in marketplace ministries. If I had another 100 years to live, this book would remain in my library. This will be a book that you read and reread; it will be a book you give to family and friends. You will find yourself going back to it for reference. It is a line upon line book. I think we are living in a day when we have a tendency to fix single meaning to truths that we have heard. In doing this, we shut ourselves out from future revelation. This is one of the most timely books I have ever had in my hand; it is a book written by a man of God whose time has come. Faithful men and women will pass this book on to faithful men and women.

Cleddie Keith
Senior Pastor, Heritage Fellowship
Florence, Kentucky

It is rare, extremely rare, to receive a living, active message from a book that changes one's life. In your hands is just such a life-shaping word to live by. The truth that makes one free is truth applied to living. My friend, Pastor Kerry Kirkwood, is a flowing "fountain head" of supernatural revelation, and *The Power of Blessing* is renewing minds and transforming hearts throughout this nation. As the Body of Christ activates the divinely given words of "Blessing," the relational principle yields the fulfillment of Jesus' high priestly prayer that we "might become one" in unity. Living out the message of *The Power of Blessing* is nothing short of *amazing*. Truly a must-read!

John H. Parks
Senior Pastor, Freedom Fellowship Church
Regional Director, Antioch Oasis International
Magnolia, Texas

Pastor Kerry has masterfully communicated these timeless truths in modern terms. With both authority and humor, *The Power of Blessing* delivers exactly what it promises—the clear understanding of what "Blessing" really means. The clear testimony of how these truths have worked in people's lives. The clear instruction of how to apply *The Power of Blessing* in our everyday lives. I consider this a must-read for every member of our congregation.

Stephen LeBlanc
Senior Pastor, Lake Country Church
Fort Worth, Texas

TABLE OF CONTENTS

INTRODUCTION

———◆———

They poured in, story after story and testimony after testimony of dramatic turnarounds in peoples' lives and situations. There was healing from physical infirmities, reconciliation in relationships, and business breakthroughs, to name a few. Hopes long gone, dreams surrendered, and prayers given up as "unanswerable" were now met, realized, and answered. These people did not just hear about the power of blessing—they put it to practice. I have witnessed firsthand the many changes in my own family and friends as a direct result of learning the power of God in blessing. This is not a theory. I have seen it work and have invested in it. Now more than ever, I am persuaded of the truth that God desires to bless man, but even more so He desires for us to bless man.

Meeting Thomas was one of those rare occasions where you know the Holy Spirit has put you on a collision course with something big. Thomas is a big man, but what would happen in the weeks ahead was bigger than both of us.

I was on my way toward the sanctuary, my usual place of prayer, when I noticed a man leaving his truck and heading for the main entrance. That entrance was locked this time of morning. The receptionist said to me, "Go on into prayer and I will take care of him." As I stepped inside the sanctuary, I felt the tug of the Holy Spirit on my heart. The impression I received was this man was sent by the Holy Spirit to see me. I greeted the man and he told me he was here to sell me some land next to the church. It was land that we definitely needed. I responded by saying we were not going to go into debt to buy any land right now.

He replied, "I will make it easy for you to pay for it."

From there he jumped into a whole new subject. He told me that he had been a pastor at one time but was asked to leave the church due to the fact that he had become a millionaire through the oilfield business. They had wanted a full-time pastor who had no other interests. His anger began to surface as he told me he had been estranged from his adult daughter for quite some time. She had moved away and his money once again became a rift. From there, Thomas told me about his young partner who he had trained and given a full partnership. The young partner was attempting to stab him in the back with other clients and take over the business. If that was not enough, he spoke of a man who tried to break up his marriage years previously.

At first I was surprised this total stranger was unfurling his life story to me. It did not take much discernment to detect the slow burn of anger coming from him. I said, "Thomas, you are doing nothing but cursing your family and business."

He was somewhat taken aback and replied, "I have gone to Bible school and I know what cussing is, and I am not cussing."

I smiled at his misunderstanding of "cursing." I said to him, "I did not say cussing as in the four-letter kind; I was referring to *cursing*."

To end our conversation, I went to our bookstore and gave him a couple of CDs on the power of blessing. He agreed to listen to them. I thought to myself that this would be the end of our short encounter. Within 24 hours, he called me back and said, "Preacher, it works. It really works."

I asked him to explain. He said, "I popped a CD into the player and listened on the way to a job site." He went on to say, "I started doing the blessing thing, and the next evening my daughter called me wanting to come home." She shared a dream she had, and in the dream a voice told her, "Call your Daddy and repent to him and go home."

He was so surprised at the quick results he decided to do the same for his business partner. Again, in a couple of days the young man came to Thomas' office and asked for forgiveness for his ungrateful attitude and confessed the conspiracy. He was seeing direct changes related to stopping the cursing and blessing instead.

The one real test was difficult. "How can I bless the man who tried to break up my home?" He knew it was God's will for him to bless, because Jesus had died for all sin for all time. He started somewhat haltingly, but soon caught the heart of the Lord. He recounted how he began to sense the wretchedness of a man who would do such a thing, and before long, compassion came over him. He even said, "If I could find the guy, instead of wanting to kill him I would give him an offering to show my forgiveness."

During the next few months, Thomas would call and give new reports of the favor of the Lord. The final blessing came later. Thomas called me, somewhat excited and somewhat perplexed. He said, "Kerry, do you remember the day I came to see you and tried to sell you some land next to the church?"

I replied, "I sure do. Like it was yesterday."

He said, "Well, I have been up half the night wrestling with God over that land. God told me that I was to give the land to your church, and I need to do it quick." Wow! We went full-circle from seeing this incredible story of Thomas being blessed, and now he blessed us with the land we needed to build the Retreat Center we had planned for many years.

Through the pages of this book, you will discover various aspects of blessing. Most of us usually think of blessing in the scope of materialism. But it is more than that. It is about a lifestyle of blessing that causes changes in the hearts of those we bless as well as ourselves. The blessing I am referring to is more along the lines of prophetic declaration. Blessing, when understood from the perspective of the Creator of the Universe, is creative and restorative. We can plainly see from the Scriptures that our Heavenly Father is the redemptive God who delights in bringing things back into His divine order. Through learning how to bless, we can participate in this redemptive process. Believers throughout time have discovered the power of blessing. They may not have articulated it in the same way, but they saw the power that lies in blessing. Though the lifestyle of blessing may be contrary to human nature, it is very much in agreement with the divine nature of God.

This book is intended to be practical in application. The reader will be able to change their perspective of life itself and how they see others. *"You will know the truth, and the truth will make you free"* (John 8:32). The reality of this verse is that the *only truth that will make us free is not the truth we hear but the truth we apply.* The subject of Truth will be a strategic part of this book.

Truth in Scripture is different from what most would call truth. The average person would probably define truth as correct information. The Bible definition is more in line with reality from God's perspective. Jesus described Himself as the *Way,* the *Truth,* and the *Life.* We can conclude that Truth is an observation from Christ's point of view.

When the 12 spies entered the land of Canaan to bring back the report of the Promised Land, they returned with various perspectives on what they saw. They reported to Moses that the land was just as God had promised. There were houses they would not have to build, vineyards they would not have to plant, and wells they would not have to dig. Ten of the spies reported that the sons of Anak were there, and they were giants. The ten referred to themselves as grasshoppers in comparison to these giants. The two other spies, Joshua and Caleb, reported the same view of the land, except they saw it through the Truth that God had said, while the others stated what they saw through only facts.

Facts are what appear in the natural, but Truth is the way things appear through the eyes of God. One of the principle points of this book is the contrast between facts and truth. Something may be factual but not necessarily truthful. God told the Israelites the land was theirs. The ones who saw the land through truth eventually were able to inherit the land. The ten who saw the promise of God through circumstantial facts only died without ever entering into their rest of inheritance. Blessing will at times seem to be factually impossible, but through truth, blessing will inherit God's intended favor.

As you read through these pages, it is my hope that you will see the importance of children receiving blessing from their fathers. Destiny, in many cases, is connected directly to the environment—whether it is one of blessing or of cursing.

My prayer is that, as you read this book, the Holy Spirit will give you understanding of this God-given ability to bless and empower you to live out this truth in every part of your life.

PART I

Revelation of
BLESSING

CHAPTER ONE

———✦———

GOOD PAINT JOB!

Marcus was an average working guy who, for the most part, was quiet in nature. He was unsuccessful in relationships, having numerous distant ones and two failed marriages. But he was a house painter by trade and was good at it.

Once, when making small talk, I asked him, "Marcus, whatever made you choose to be a house painter?"

Surprisingly, his reply was rather definite—he told the story like it was part of his diary. He said, "My dad was a salesman who traveled most of the time and was only home on weekends. When he came home, that was the time when he told me all of my mistakes from the previous week and my instructions for correcting them. It seemed like I never did anything that gained his approval. His harsh criticism wore heavy on me most of the time. But one weekend would set my destiny for life. I had built a birdhouse and was finishing the paint job when my dad walked in. He looked at me, glanced at the birdhouse, and said, 'Good paint job!' His words of blessing and approval gave me a level of confidence I had never received from him before. This guided me to believing that I could paint houses and get paid for it." Talk about certainty!

But not all of us have a "light bulb moment" like Marcus, where, in one definite instant, we are certain about our direction in life. Most of us will have an accumulation of words or penetrating truths (whether those are internal deposits or an external course) that shape our lives and steer us toward a career or the lack thereof.

A parent, a close friend, or a relative can have such a great impact in our formation. The impact of these experiences will vary in degree, depending on the weightiness of the relationship. Even then, knowing our calling and destiny can be a struggle. It is enough of a struggle that many pass through life without ever really knowing why on earth they were placed here.

There is a calling greater than any profession we choose. It is even greater than being called an apostle, prophet, evangelist, pastor, teacher, or any other spiritual gift. Peter's letter makes this calling clear.

> *Finally, all of you be of one mind, having compassion for one another; love as brothers, **be tenderhearted, be courteous; not returning evil for evil or reviling for reviling, but on the contrary blessing, knowing that you were called to this, that you may inherit a blessing*** (1 Peter 3:8-9 NKJV).

Simple and uncomplicated, but filled with expectation. What we are called to do is to bless and to receive the blessing. Discovering the power that is in blessing will open up a whole new world of thinking and living. Blessing and its counterpart, cursing, will set a path for us without our being fully aware of it.

The word "called" (*kaleo*) is a strong word that carries the same significance as choosing a person's name.[1] It is similar to asking a parent of a newborn baby, "What are you going to call him?" We name children for the purpose of distinction and identification. In many cultures, the name is prophetic for the child's future. Naming and even nicknaming children is marking them in faith. Basically we are saying over them, "This is your destiny and it is who you are," or "This is the value of your life." The name God gave Jesus is a *called* name.

For this reason also, God highly exalted Him, and bestowed on Him the name which is above every name, so that at the name of Jesus every knee will bow, of those who are in Heaven and on earth and under the earth (Philippians 2:9-10).

Jesus was named and marked for the purpose of blessing and for the defending of those cursed. He became the Savior of God's creation from the curse.

Making It Plain

"God bless you!"

People say that all the time and consider that to be blessing someone. Not really. It's more than that. Saying "Bless you," has become such a common salutation or spiritual filler for any occasion that the power of blessing is lost and remains untapped. Blessing is not one-dimensional, as in the accumulation of material assets. Someone saying, "I have been blessed with a big house or car," is acknowledging only one dimension of it. But blessing is not one-sided where we are just the recipients of it. Another side to blessing is veiled from the casual observer. "Blessing" in the Bible is one of those words that is filled with meaning, like the word "peace" or "grace," depending on how it is used.

More than a mere formality, blessing has the power to turn lives around and make us into a blesser. Let's back track to the Old Testament where the word "blessing" there is the Hebrew word *barak*. This simply means, "to speak the intention of God," and "to be happy with where you are."[2] In the New Testament, it is the word *eulogia* from which we get the word "eulogy." *Eulogia* means "to speak larger or well of," or "to speak the intention or favor of God on someone."[3] Just as eulogies are tailormade, so are blessings.

True blessing spoken over someone or something is describing the way God sees them. This is a prophetic insight to see the way someone or something is supposed to be, not how they may appear to be at the moment. Therefore, when we talk about blessing someone, we are prophetically stating: "May the

Lord grant you all of His intention for you," or, "May God's full expectation for you be fulfilled in your life." And we know that God's intentions for people are good. Take a short trip to Jeremiah 29:11, or revisit the first few chapters of Genesis—these speak of the heart of God toward us, His creation.

When we speak blessings over our children as Jacob did, we are saying what their life should be (see Gen. 49:1-28). Jacob was not stating the condition of his children at the moment but what they would be. If you follow Jacob's sons throughout Scripture, it is obvious they followed the prophetic path of the blessing from their father. The idea of blessing has nothing to do with whether they are walking it out at that moment or not. Understanding this truth eliminates our tendency to act as the judge or the jury of whether someone is deserving of blessing.

God's intentions are not contingent on whether the recipient has the right attitude, either. It has nothing to do with how we feel and everything to do with how God wants it to be. When we declare God's intentions, we release His ability to change things from what they are into His desired plan. What a radically different response from what we naturally tend to do! We tend to overstate the problem without stating any of God's intended plans. It's no surprise when our prayers are more of a reporting nature than praying the solution. We are good at reporting the doctor's diagnosis, the conditions surrounding a situation, and so on. Precious time is wasted when we continually rehearse the disaster that will occur if God does not come through in a situation. It's with the *eyes of faith* that we look at the situation through God's perspective.

THE FAITH FACTOR

Speaking of faith, let's check out Proverbs.

> *A faithful man will* ***abound*** *with blessings...* (Proverbs 28:20).

We usually interpret this as a faithful man will receive blessing. But the sentence structure means that a man of faith will be full of blessing. To be "full of blessing" means that the blessing is in us to give away. We receive it from the Father so we can give it out. We cannot give away what we don't have. And if God says we can bless, then it must be in us to give. The same thing is true with forgiveness. Like blessing, it is a gift that we can either give or withhold.

It's a spiritual principle. Whatever we sow will set a measurement of return. Needing mercy from God? Then give mercy. Want blessing? Release blessing. Asking God for blessing and then withholding it from others hinders us from receiving it ourselves. First Peter 3:9 finishes up by saying that we are not to return insult for insult. Giving insults for some people is a national pastime; they seem to be invigorated by insult exchanges. The same is true with cursing. If we give insults we get insulted. Cursing people while in traffic sets a measure where we will be more stalled in traffic. Or if we are asking for something evil to happen to someone and we rejoice when it does, then we should not be surprised when we are in difficult places.

> *He who withholds grain, the people will curse him, but blessing will come on the head of him who sells it* (Proverbs 11:26).

What's the idea here? If I want blessing, I have to develop a lifestyle of blessing others. In Proverbs 28:20, *abounding* is a picture of a reservoir or storage and in many cases refers to water. We are created to be a reservoir of life-sustaining encouragement. Later in Chapter Three we will dig deeper into this concept.

A person who is full of faith will have the ability to bless continually. Why? Becoming a blesser is an issue of faith, because when we bless we are doing it through faith. Human nature is resistant to blessing others. This becomes more difficult when we come across people who continually take blessings and never give them. Oh, but how we love to hang around those who do bless! Thankfully, that natural tendency can be overcome by looking to our perfect example—Jesus Christ. He blessed the tax collectors and sinners who were looked down upon by society and even children who were considered less important. By being a blesser, Jesus repelled every demonic force that came against Him because in

Him there was no curse. Even though people spat on Him, pulled His beard, and hung Him on the Cross, He refused to curse; instead, He blessed them. He was moving toward them in the opposite spirit.

Being filled with the faith to bless comes from hearing the Word of God.

> *Faith comes from hearing and hearing by the word...* (Romans 10:17).

Faith and belief are not the same. Beliefs are formed from what we were trained and taught, and they create a foundation or a structure of values. Faith is the "now" and it comes by hearing. What we are hearing now produces faith, not what we heard 20 years ago, because that can wane with time. Faith is knowing—inside our spirit at a particular moment—God's desire and will for someone or something. We can then move to align ourselves with God's perspective. The knowing produces in us a readiness to speak the Lord's mind for that person or situation. We can know God's will for an individual or situation without being on our faces in prayer for 30 minutes! Though the specifics for the individual are not revealed, we do know God's general will through the written Word of God. The written Word becomes our repertoire for blessing. (I'll explain more in Chapter Six.) This eliminates being worried about whether we are doing it right. Knowing God's revealed will creates confidence in prayer that God hears us (see Matt. 21:22).

No wonder the book of Hebrews tells us that it is impossible to please God without faith (see Heb. 11:6). Faith is agreement with God's perspective. Without question, seeing someone's potential through the eyes of God makes it easier to bless. Faith is essential to releasing the power of blessing.

INHERITED BLESSINGS

Martita's family inheritance was tied up in dispute after dispute. It was like "The Family Feud." The large amount of land could not be sold because of the vehement disagreements. Among her siblings, the situation was a messy affair.

The rivalry had lasted for a long period of time. Way too long. The lawyers were not able to help in the disbursing of the settlement. No one had told her that receiving an inheritance would be this complicated and divisive.

Martita listened intently as I taught on the power that was in blessing. Obviously, her family needed it. Just as the truth about blessing was sinking in, God showed her a picture of a web that had been spun and was entangling her siblings. It was time to kill the spider of cursing and untangle its web from around her family's inheritance through blessing. So she began by considering what the Lord would speak over her family. She consistently blessed her rivaling siblings, even in the face of their resistance to God's intentions for their lives and children. Within a few days, the call came. They were ready to settle in an agreeable fashion. Blessing took Martita from months of heartache and pain to a resolution in a matter of days.

There is an inheritance that can be passed on through blessing. The last part of First Peter 3:9 concluded that, *"...you were called for the very purpose that you might inherit a blessing."* This verse infers that through blessing we can come into our inheritance. Parents can leave their children a legacy of blessing or cursing. I believe that natural and spiritual inheritances are held up until we learn not to repay evil for evil or insult for insult. Blessing frees up our inheritance.

We see this in the case of Esau and Jacob. Esau the firstborn had the blessing of the birthright.

> *When Jacob had cooked stew, Esau came in from the field and he was famished; and Esau said to Jacob, "Please let me have a swallow of that red stuff there, for I am famished." Therefore his name was called Edom. But Jacob said, "First sell me your birthright." Esau said, "Behold, I am about to die; so of what use then is the birthright to me?" And Jacob said, "First swear to me"; so he swore to him, and sold his birthright to Jacob. Then Jacob gave Esau bread and lentil stew; and he ate and drank, and rose and went on his way. Thus Esau despised his birthright* (Genesis 25:29-34).

Jacob was not a blesser at this point. Instead of giving the soup to his brother, he sold it to him for his birthright. Esau's response was as bad as Jacob's deception. Not only did he despise the inherited blessing that was his from his parents, but he also cursed his brother Jacob. Later, we find in Scripture that some tough words were used to describe that fateful transaction for Esau.

> *There be no **immoral or godless** person like Esau, who sold his own birthright for a single meal. For you know that even afterwards, **when he desired to inherit the blessing,** he was rejected, for he found no place for repentance, though he sought for it with tears* (Hebrews 12:16-17).

By that act, Esau revealed that he did not value his position or birthright.

How about this verse?

> *Just as it is written, "Jacob I loved, but Esau I hated"* (Romans 9:13).

Wow! What a strong statement! The word *hate* there means "to be hot against." God hates that spirit that causes us to despise blessing others.[4]

By despising his birth position, Esau cursed it. He was willing to sell it for a pot of stew, and though he repented and sought it, he could not find a place to be restored to it. He was duped, because at that moment he thought he was going to die and was not going to need it. If he had only recognized that the birthright was a position of blessing, power, and strength!

Rejecting our call to bless is despising the blessing. The blessing enables us to become part of the inheritance of those who were blessed, like the blessing that is on Israel. Being grafted in as Christians brings that blessing to us. It's like adoption. We did not have a right to that family, but now we do.

Blessing is also a form of worship. When we choose to bless we are acknowledging that God's view of someone is greater than our own opinion. Similarly, we bless our food as a way of acknowledging that it was a gift from

God. The Lord receives the act of blessing as a declaration of His heart. That becomes a glimpse of the divine nature of our Heavenly Father for the world.

OPEN HAND

God blesses us so that we can be a blessing. Isn't that what the Lord said to Abraham?

> *Now the Lord had said to Abram: "Get out of your country, from your family and from your father's house, to a land that I will show you. I will make you a great nation;* **I will bless you and make your name great; and you shall be a blessing. I will bless those who bless you,** *and I will curse him who curses you; and in you all the families of the earth shall be blessed"* (Genesis 12:1-3 NKJV).

The New Testament revealed a man who had the ability to bless but would not do it.

> *Now behold, one came and said to Him, "Good Teacher, what good thing shall I do that I may have eternal life?" So He said to him, "Why do you call Me good? No one is good but One, that is, God. But if you want to enter into life, keep the commandments." He said to Him, "Which ones?" Jesus said, "'You shall not murder,' 'You shall not commit adultery,' 'You shall not steal,' 'You shall not bear false witness,' 'Honor your father and your mother,' and, 'You shall love your neighbor as yourself.'" The young man said to Him, "All these things I have kept from my youth. What do I still lack?" Jesus said to him, "If you want to be perfect, go, sell what you have and give to the poor, and you will have treasure in Heaven; and come, follow Me." But when the young man heard that saying, he went away sorrowful, for he had great possessions* (Matthew 19:16-22 NKJV).

The word "sell" there is the word *poleo,* which doesn't mean to get rid of all your possessions.[5] It means to "go and do business and take what you get from that business and give to the poor." In other words, give out of what you receive from your bartering and trading. Jesus knew that the young man had the ability to bless the poor. But the ruler saw wealth as a means of increasing his own influence, not something to part with. Give his profits to the poor? No way! He could not do it. So he went away sad. What he wanted was Jesus' approval, but what he got was instruction to do something he refused to do.

The power of blessing is working inside us. When we don't bless, this power lays dormant. We just become recipients of blessing. We can have plenty of stuff like the rich young ruler, but we are not happy because we were designed by God to be blessers. Our greatest joy is when we are sowing the intentions of God. Any unhappiness with our body, marriage, children, or pastor is due to us not blessing them. By blessing, we receive God's intended goodness toward us in full capacity, including long life and healthy relationships. We become partakers or partners of what and whom we are blessing. That act also gives the Holy Spirit an even stronger leadership through our lives. It then becomes a lifestyle of obedience.

If a painter's destiny could be directed by his earthly father's acknowledgment of a job well done, how much more would our Heavenly Father want to acknowledge the good things that He has for us? Understanding our calling to be blessers causes us to live more purposeful lives. Releasing blessing moves us closer to our intended destiny, and our lives will display patterns of fullness and success. By this, we further show the world God's generous heart.

PRAYER

Father, I really want to bless and be a person of blessing. I want to walk in the power of Your Spirit. I know the price for that and it is not too difficult, nor is it far away. It is right in my mouth.

Cause me, Lord, to become a blesser in this city, even as You said that You blessed Abraham so that he could become a blessing to all the families of the earth. Father, I ask that You would "touch my lips," as Isaiah said, with coals from off the altar, that I may become a mouthpiece and speak as a person called and sent from God to bless.

Deliver me from evil and deliver me from cursing for Your name's sake, so that I might enter into the inheritance that You have already given.

ENDNOTES

1. Biblesoft's New Exhaustive Strong's Numbers and Concordance with Expanded Greek-Hebrew Dictionary. CD-ROM. Biblesoft, Inc. and International Bible Translators, Inc., s.v. *kaleo* (NT 2564).

2. Strong's s.v. *barak* (1288).

3. Strong's s.v. *eulogia* (2127).

4. Strong's s.v. *miseo* (3404).

5. Strong's s.v. *poleo* (4160).

Chapter Two

—❧—

Blessing versus Cursing

Remember the days when we thought that if God would get rough enough, then people would turn to the Lord? I never found that to be true.

But I grew up hearing my mother pray for my father this way: "Lord, just dangle him over the flames and let him feel the heat of hell."

And feel it he did, and so did our family!

So one day I asked her, "Why don't you pray the peace of God on him so we can get some peace ourselves?"

Thank God, she finally did.

What's New?

Mom did not know it at the time, and neither do some Christians. Asking God to turn up the heat on someone so they will repent rarely works. God defends the cursed under the new covenant. This new covenant truth runs counter to what many Christians are taught.

If we curse someone, God will withstand us even if the one we cursed is not a good person. Cursing puts us in opposition to the reason Jesus came to die.

> *Christ redeemed us from the curse of the Law, having become a curse for us—for it is written, "Cursed is everyone who hangs on a tree"* (Galatians 3:13).

When I set a standard of cursing or speaking evil toward others, then God, by His own nature and righteousness, will defend the one I cursed. I can then find myself opposing God. Isn't that interesting? If someone curses you, God will defend you even if He doesn't agree with what you are doing.

God is a father. A father does not want other people to say bad things about their children or get on them for doing wrong. Now, the father of the child may want to get on them for doing wrong, but he doesn't want you to do it. As a parent, you will defend your children to the fullest degree. In the same manner, God will defend the cursed, even against a sibling.

Proclaiming the good news is staking the claim of Jesus. He came to release people from their pain and not to tell people how deep they are in sin.

> *The Spirit of the Lord is upon me, because He anointed me to preach the gospel to the poor. He has sent me to* **proclaim** *release to the captives, and recovery of sight to the blind, to set free those who are oppressed* (Luke 4:18).

The word "proclaim" in that verse is broken in two words: *Pro* means to advance, and *claim* means "a right to something, or to assert and demand the recognition of a right, title, or possession." Proclaim means "to advance the claim." In the previous verse, it means to proclaim God's goodness and mercy and favor in a situation. Blessing is proclaiming this truth and the intentions of God over our families and all that concerns us.

Jesus fulfilled Luke 4:18. His life on earth was given to the preaching of the good news, healing, and delivering the oppressed. He forgave sins. Even the sins of the woman who was caught in the act of adultery and deserved punishment according to the law (see John 8:3-5;7-11)! Forgiving her did not mean that Jesus was agreeing with her sin. Rather, He stopped the curse on her life by telling her to go and sin no more. Jesus' mission was to save the world, not condemn it. And with His life, He delivered humankind from the curse. It was a complete work and it was enough.

SAME VOICE

The prophet Amos wrote, *"Can two walk together, unless they are agreed?"* (Amos 3:3 NKJV). Being in agreement with someone is *yawad,* to say the same thing or to meet together.[1] Agreement is vital for any relationship. Our idea of agreement is that we cannot agree if we do not feel the same way. But that is not God's way of agreement. His is on a higher level. Agreement with God is to say what He is saying. We do not have to feel the same way He does. Just because we feel the same way as someone else does not mean that we are in agreement.

Am I being a hypocrite, then, if I'm blessing someone when I want something bad to happen instead? Certainly not! I don't have to agree with what they are doing or with what I'm blessing. I am simply agreeing with God. Feelings can change, but God's Word does not. Blessing is agreement with the Word of the Lord, and that truth remains regardless of feelings or situations.

I've been in conversations where someone would say, "Well, I think God should do this."

My reply was, "What does the Word of God say?"

It disarmed them, especially if they know what God's Word says. The point is this—what I think is not invalid, but agreeing with what God is saying is more important.

Agreeing with God is standing and declaring His will "on earth as it is in Heaven." That is being on His side.

*But the hour is coming, and now is, when the true worshipers will worship the Father in spirit and truth; for the Father is seeking such to **worship** Him* (John 4:23 NKJV).

The word *worship* is very similar to "blessing." Since God is seeking true worshipers, we can say that He is also seeking blessers. He seeks blessers who will bless the name of the Lord and those He created to worship Him. He is seeking people on earth to declare what He is expressing in Heaven.

UNMASKING CURSES

Man's fallen nature tends to oppose blessing. When questioned by God as to why he was hiding, Adam's first response was to blame Eve, which in actuality was blaming God for giving him a woman like her. Eve, in turn, blamed her sin on the devil (see Gen. 3:9-13). Our very fallen nature is to blame others for our condition.

We are either blessing or cursing. There is no neutral ground. God is the Blesser and the devil is the curser, or the "accuser of the brethren."

> *Then I heard a loud voice in Heaven, saying, "Now the salvation, and the power, and the Kingdom of our God and the authority of His Christ have come, for the **accuser of our brethren** has been thrown down, he who accuses them before our God day and night"* (Revelation 12:10).

Curses are not just confined to speaking evil words over people. The following are constituted as curses.

Accusations are a curse. Most people do not want to commit sin. The reason why most people do is because they are under a curse and their eyes are blind. But it is possible for someone under constant accusations to come to a place where they begin to agree with accusations. Agreement with accusations is a yield sign for sin. I have had people say to me that since they were accused of something all their life they might as well do it. By agreeing and operating under the accusations, they in turn begin to accuse others, and a curse becomes part of their lives.

Withholding God's heart and intention for someone is also a curse. Someone's negative actions or attitude toward us is not even an excuse (no matter how justified we feel about it) to deny them blessing. We can take on their spirit by withholding any affection, blessing, or love which is due them. So, when a husband withholds blessings from his wife, his prayers can literally be hindered.

> *Husbands, likewise, dwell with them with understanding, giving honor to the wife, as to the weaker vessel, and as being heirs together of the grace of life, that your prayers may not be hindered* (1 Peter 3:7 NKJV).

This is not permission for a woman to use that Scripture against her husband. God places great value in our treatment and attitude toward each other—especially of those in our own households!

It is also a curse to speak anything contrary to God's will or intention over someone. After all, it's our opinion against God's. So to say that someone will not amount to anything or to recount their failures are acts that fall into the cursing category. Though we may pride ourselves for having an opinion about everything, this habit brings us in agreement with the accuser. Being opinionated is a difficult habit to quit.

You see, it is possible to live a mediocre life while cursing people. However, the life of joy and blessing comes from those who bless. Cursing reveals that the heart is full of bitterness and resentment which will flow out of the mouth. We may never call for divination on anyone, but we can certainly curse them with these kinds of words and attitudes. The truth of the matter is cursing affects us more than the one we may be cursing. Have you ever heard any one use this form of expression? "I'll tell you what, if they ever catch on fire, I'll not walk across the street and spit on them to put them out. But I'm not going to say anything bad about them."

Unfortunately, the fallen nature of man is to curse or speak evil against those who did it to us. Ever heard of people saying, "I can tell them off in a heartbeat"? One may walk away feeling good and think, "Boy, I sure told them off," but at that moment they have entered into agreement with the cursing. We may win a battle of words but lose the entire war of living in the favor of the Lord.

Curses cannot land without a cause (see Prov. 26:2). The blood of Jesus is our covering from them. Still, certain things can open the door to a curse. Fear is one. Fear is an evident token to the enemy of a falling away, and it empowers a curse. Severe emotional wounding is another, like wounds from extreme violations such as molestation, rape, and incest. Agreeing with accusations and having faith in them are also invitations to a curse. By mulling over lies, we can literally receive them into our spirits and allow a curse to take root. Curses spread just like rumors—by someone agreeing and believing that lie. Those who indulge in cursing have built a landing pad for curses to alight and build strongholds.

Despising prophetic utterances is another avenue for curses. This path is often overlooked. We do not prophesy so we can say we are prophetic. Prophecy is all about blessing people. For us, to despise prophetic blessing as Esau despised his birthright is to despise the blessing of the Lord. I am not referring to so-called prophecy that does not edify or speak of the heart of Christ for His Bride.

When we curse others, we align ourselves with the accuser. Sometimes that manifests in our bank account shrinking or difficulties in our relationships and an overall lack of favor upon our lives. Constantly feeling rejected or being easily offended can also be a sign of habitual cursing flowing through us. Perhaps we are unknowingly cursing a spouse, child, boss, or person in authority, for example.

For many of us, we assume God feels the same way we do. We like to believe that God thinks the way we think. If we don't like it, then He must not like it. Joshua, Moses' successor, had the same perspective.

Now it came about when Joshua was by Jericho, that he lifted up his eyes and looked, and behold, a man was standing opposite him with his sword drawn in his hand, and Joshua went to him and said to him, "Are you for us or for our adversaries?" He said, "No; rather I indeed come now as captain of the host of the Lord" (Joshua 5:13-14).

Joshua wanted to know which side the angel's sword would stand with. The angel said that he was neither, but he was on the Lord's side, which stands for righteousness and the blessing of the Lord.

The issue with blessing is not whether we agree with someone on how things are to be done. God is not a Democrat or Republican. He is not telling us to stand on the sidelines of the issues, but He calls us to bless and not curse.

Some time ago, my wife, Diane, and I were in France ministering in a leadership retreat. While on the lunch break, a middle-aged Frenchman sat across from us and began a casual conversation in good English. He quickly wanted to know why the United States did not do more to solve "global warming." It was obvious he wanted to pull me into a debate and take me out of the place of rest. He was disarmed when his insults about my country met with me returning blessing over his. Although I was ready to defend this country that I love with my own political views, I have to realize that God is not American or French. He is God of all. It is difficult to understand, sometimes, why we should bless when ungodly people do terrible things. The answer is a simple one—because the nature of God-likeness is to bless and not curse or enter into cursing with others who do.

Blessing is not about sides. God is not against us. This is not to say that we should neglect positions of righteousness, but even at times where people are clearly in the wrong, we can still bless them. Blessing is about seeing what God intends to happen, not the way it is at the moment.

Don't get caught up in the hostility and the polarization that is happening in our society, where we cannot communicate with people because they don't have the same affiliation we do. That is exactly what satan wants—division and polarization. Blessing breaches division and injects the spirit of Christ into the situation. The media promote and spew out cursing, much to the devil's delight! Resist being pulled into those dialogues, and instead let a prophetic heart show what God would really intend for the situation. When our eyes are on Jesus, we can intercede and bless whoever is in authority in a nation. We want to answer the call to pray and bless. In this way, we can resist the spirit of confusion that has come upon the nation and the Church.

The devil always wants us to take sides. We may see people that are not affiliated with our group or denomination and we begin to complain or act self-righteous. "Lord, they are out there prophesying! They are not part of us." "They don't do church like we do." "They don't believe the same way we do." It was similar in Moses' time. Numbers 11 tells the account of two guys named Eldad and Medad who were prophesying among the camp of Israel. Joshua, a young man at that point, suggested to Moses that he restrain them because they were not part of their recognized group. Moses in his wisdom replied to Joshua, *"Are you jealous for my sake?"* He said, *"Would that all the Lord's people were prophets…"* (Num. 11:29). What a wonderful sight to behold if all of God's would bless those they had contact with!

Pressures to take sides in matters do come. I've had my fair share of them. Situations have happened where people in my life urged me to take a particular side. My refusal only stirred their anger. How could I be their friend and not be on their side, cursing their offender? Whose side was I on anyway? As a follower of Christ, I am not to choose your side or their side, but I am to be on God's side. Friends may want you on their side, but a friend of God stands on the side of God. As your friend, you need me to be blessing you and not just to be on your side. It is possible to be on the wrong side. One thing I do know is that the only side God favors is the side committed to blessing.

People become angry with God because of unanswered prayers or unfulfilled hopes. It never occurs to them that God may have desired to do it, but cursing has held up the answers they have looked for. Remember First Peter 3:7, which exhorts husbands and wives to live in such a way that their prayers are not hindered. God does not contradict His own Kingdom principle of bless and be blessed, curse and be cursed.

Knowing God's revealed will through His Word keeps us from stumbling around in the dark when it comes to blessing. Our trip down a path that opposes God can stop too. And it's worth the 180-degree turn that many of us will make when we see the benefits of blessing—the disarming of accusers, closing the door to the enemy, and fulfilling the word of God.

PRAYER

Father, I come and present myself before You as an instrument of blessing. I want to be an oracle, a mouthpiece to blessing. Lord, give me the vocabulary so that I turn away from being so quick to curse and speak evil of people and instead bless them. Give me the words to bless those that I don't even know and to honor the dignitaries you have placed in authority over my life.

I speak grace over my children. I see the situation not as insurmountable or destructive, but I see it with the eyes of grace. I see what can be. Lord, help me not to have a narrow mind and a mind so shut that I cannot hear You. Spirit of the Lord, help me right now. Bring me to a place of maturity, so that the power that works within me is not self-destructive but one where I am proclaiming the blessing of others so that I might be blessed.

ENDNOTE

1. Biblesoft's New Exhaustive Strong's Numbers and Concordance with Expanded Greek-Hebrew Dictionary. CD-ROM. Biblesoft, Inc. and International Bible Translators, Inc., s.v. *yawad* (NT 3259).

PART II

Inclusion for
BLESSING

Chapter Three

❧

Apple of God's Eye

He possessed it—this wondrous ability to foresee. This time, the promised reward was glorious. If nobody ever paid him again to prophecy, he would still be set for life, reveling in this luxury. God must be really happy with him. Balaam's head was still spinning with this good fortune as he prepared his donkey for the journey. He never saw that his newest assignment was going to be the death of his own desire for fame and riches. Now, where was that donkey?

Elsewhere in the land a people camped, oblivious to the summoning of the most revered pagan prophet at the time, called to recite their fate. They had journeyed far from Egypt to embrace what was promised them—a land flowing with goodness. Eyes always on this promise of God, their hearts often faltered. Yet they clung to the hope that they were the "apple of God's eye," and their destiny was not too far off.

Turning away his head from the campsite below, Balak was not smiling. What he saw made his heart tremble. A multitude spread out on his backyard as far as his eye could see (see Num. 22:2-3). Military might and numbers were not this people's weakness. Having their women, children, and possessions with them seemed to only heighten their vigilance to protect their own. Rumors said that everything went well for this people—unless, of course, their God was mad at them. Well, if it was the supernatural on which this people relied for help, then he, Balak, could call on the same source to defeat them. He felt a little at ease as he peered into the distance for signs of relief. Balak tried to remember his message to the prophet.

> *Now, therefore, please come, curse this people for me since they are too mighty for me; perhaps I may be able to defeat them and drive them out of the land. For I know that he whom you bless is blessed, and he whom you curse is cursed* (Numbers 22:6).

He could hardly wait for the prophet to show up.

But the next day brought no good news for Balak. The stubborn prophet had refused to come. The elders had reported that the prophet had simply stated that *"...the Lord has refused to let me go with you"* (Num. 22:13). Was it a spiritual cover-up to say the divination fee was too low, or perhaps the messengers were not distinguished enough? (See Numbers 22:15.) Did Balaam not understand that Balak had the power to honor the prophet in ways he could only dream of? (See Numbers 22:37.) No way were the Moabites going to be added to the list of nations that the Israelites humiliated! He needed to up the price and the distinction of the delegates. This time, the soothsayer would be a fool not to come.

Balaam was stumped. God had said no. Sounds awfully familiar, doesn't it? Did God not want him to prosper? He had sadly watched as his wealth rode away in the morning dust with the Moabite and Midianite elders. What was so important to God about slaves fleeing from Egypt anyway? God did not explain very much. For now, he had to be content with what God said: *"Do not go with them; you shall not curse the people, for they are blessed"* (Num. 22:12). We've all been there—those moments when God puts a screeching halt on our plans and projects. From our point of view, the whole deal appeared to be a blessing until God put the brakes on it. Or was it?

The prophet's dilemma was far from over. Later that day, he hosted another Midianite and Moabite surprise party. Such a persistent lot! And then the real kicker—God had agreed to let him go, on the condition that he would only say what God told him to say (see Num. 22:20). How hard could that be? Extremely difficult, when we consider the fact that Balaam had to choose between repeating God's promptings or kiss his fee goodbye. Then the thought hit him. If God could change His mind about his going, then He surely could change His mind about other things, too. He wondered how much leeway he had.

All too soon, Balaam was reminded that God was against this trip in the first place. It began when his faithful and trusty donkey took a detour on its own accord. Striking the animal got it back on track but then it crushed Balaam's foot against the wall. Now what? More beating followed, but the donkey refused to budge and plopped down on the spot. Utterly frustrated, Balaam began to beat the beast. And then the donkey started to talk. Without even thinking this a strange phenomena, the prophet is having a conversation with his donkey.

Opening Balaam's eyes so he could see the angel prevented more humiliation for the eager prophet and prevented God from having to listen to Balaam talk with his donkey. The prophet was saved from death by his animal! He was repentant before the angel. This was a divine checkpoint for Balaam. God made sure that Balaam understood that for him to pass through, he was to say only God's words and desires—not Balak's or Balaam's. There was zero room for profit or flattering words for gain. He died there that day, in a sense. Balaam died to his will and abandoned any ambition about the whole matter. "... *The word that God puts in my mouth, that I shall speak"* (Num. 22:38). God could finally trust him.

SIGHTING THE PRIZE

How so many of us are like Balaam! We glue our sights on fame and fortune and become confused when the "donkeys" in our lives speak. Oh yes, we will ask God for His will, but then our own will captures our hearts more. Opposition from God may arise against our plans, but we are too focused on them to even pay attention. Even when our feet are smashed against the wall of life, we beat the "donkey" in frustration until that moment when our eyes open, and we realize that we had been resistant to God's will to bless. Worse still, we could have died in our selfish ambitions and hard-heartedness! Then we see our own hearts and not-so-godly motives and we cringe inwardly. Thank God for the donkeys! We finally seem to get it. We see the angel, and we surrender our mouths to God. Suddenly, our prophetic destiny that was stuck somewhere between Heaven and earth is released, and we are released to move forward.

Straining against God's word, our bad attitudes and wrong mind-sets trip us up every time. These bad attitudes may be admirable in the world, but they lack luster with God. Boasting, "I'm going to give them a piece of my mind first and then tell them what God told me to say!" never gets the results we long for. Our attitude of "telling it like I see it" may get us pats on the back, but the fruit is bitter and unpleasant. A little pinch of God, a dash of cursing, then mixing it with blessing does not get us the prize. To collect on God's favor we have to agree on God's terms.

Ever struggled with the knowledge that it is God's will to bless you, but you are not experiencing any of the promise? Feeling like a second-class citizen or someone outside the loop, you have a nagging suspicion that something is amiss. Going through the mental checklist, we may find that we did speak God's blessings, but then we added our two cents. Those two cents were sort of a freebie to coax them along the way, but it sure was not God. Then we ride away on the donkey and we run into Him. God was not going to let us get away with half-hearted commitments. He is not being mean; He just wanted complete control of our willingness to bless—for our own good. Balaam's heart had to be fully devoted to the Lord, and we are required no less.

GETTING THERE

Balaam arrived to a celebration given by the Moabite king. The real test began the next day. Hustling the prophet up to the high place, Balak figures that a visual of the *"horde"* who *"cover the surface of the land"* would help

Balaam (see Num. 22:4-5). Would the prophet falter at the pressure to please either this distressed king or the God that let him come? Then Balaam did what he knew was the right thing to do—he built the altars, prepared the sacrifice, and then tuned his ear to God (see Num. 23:1-4).

Arriving to the "there" is the real test. Sometimes the setup is not the way we envisioned. No soft music is playing, there's no welcome committee, no intercessors are praying, and there are no signs of God. We may find chaos, an irritable person or two, unfavorable conditions, and pressure to conform. Or a trickier scenario is when the eagerness of those waiting for us becomes a temptation to say more than what God told us to say. Whatever the setup, if our heart surrendered to God prior to that time, we can be at peace. God always meets us.

Up on the hill, the Lord delivered to the prophet's ear the message. Balaam trudged back to find Balak and his leaders, positioned and waiting for Balaam's word. What he said, in effect, caused Balak great concern.

"OK, so you wanted me to curse this people for you? No way is that going to happen! God has blessed them. From up here, I'm trying to see something bad about these people, but there's nothing. Yeah, they live apart from everybody else and no one thinks much of them. But hey, just wait until these people grow! How I wish that I end up like them!"

Balak was not quite sure he heard correctly, but the gaping mouths of his elders were evidence enough. "Hey! What are you doing to me? I brought you here to curse them, not bless them!"

"Just trying to obey God," piped the prophet.

"It must be the angle from which Balaam was observing the Israelites," thought Balak. "How gullible can the prophet be! Just one survey of the massive migrants and their goods and he is impressed!" But then Balak sighed. He himself wavered between two thoughts—admiration for this people who put themselves in the hands of an unseen God, or anger at their idiocy. "Maybe if Balaam had just observed a portion of them, hmm, that might do it." He knew a spot from which these people won't look so good. Nothing looks terrible like the struggling stragglers of a multitude. There was no visible glory there.

Guiding Balaam to the new location where he could spy on the trespassers, Balak was pleased—this was a good view. Why, they did not look that grand from there! He glanced over at the prophet limping away to be alone with God. That troubled him somewhat. He hoped this was not the same God that the Israelites trusted. It couldn't be! Didn't Balaam come from Pethor of Mesopotamia? With a furrowed brow, he reasoned that cursing a part of the lot was better than none. After all, how many good things can you see in people, especially ones you don't know? For now, he just had to pretend that Balaam did not bless his enemies earlier. "Patience, Balak," he told himself, "patience."

Such a picture of our soul's enemy! Balak's determination to curse even a portion of the Israelites revealed an old trick of the enemy. Ever so subtle, his desire is to at least get his toe in the door or his thumb in the window, and then the weight follows. Familiarizing himself with our bad and weak spots, he loves to highlight those flaws. He hopes that if we look long enough at the dark side of life, we will begin to talk about it. Isn't that normal human nature?

Think about offenses—because they hurt, they whine for attention. They get us fixated on the wrongs of another. So while we cradle the wound with our sight, we may overlook the offender's relationship to the whole. But the devil does not forget it. Our cursing the mother-in-law, for instance, appears to spare our spouse from harm, but we forget she is still part of the family. Just as we are linked by blood, the laws of God connect the givers and receivers of the cursing and blessing. Never will the devil want us to look through God's eyes. Even one peek can be enough to breathe in us life and hope. Failing to prevent that one glance, the devil will work to distort and twist that view until we doubt that we saw anything at all.

Hindsight might be 20-20, but the view from a blesser's side is better than from anywhere else. We all know too well how our view (and opinions) of life and others determine our thoughts and words. Developing a cursing mentality is easy and subtle. Though our heart's desire may be to bless, if our sights are set on cursing, it is almost guaranteed that cursing will come out. A cursing environment has a way of sucking us into it if we are staring at it. If we are not careful, we can be like Balak, thinking, "Hey, I'm the victim here! They started it!" Redirecting our eyes to match God's gaze is ongoing. It is possible to have and see good come out of situations. That would mean finding out what God is seeing in someone or something. These tried and tested words remain ever so true, *"Where there is no vision* (prophetic revelation) *the people are unrestrained* (have nothing to tie themselves to)" (Prov. 29:18). Those revelations become our anchor for living a fulfilling life.

Bringing It Home

Lending his ears and eyes to the Lord's words, Balaam became another voice to confirm the goodness of God toward a nation. The donkey had done its work. Balaam delivered another punch to the Moabite king's ego.

> *God is not a man, that He should lie, nor a son of man, that He should repent; has He said, and will He not do it? Or has He spoken, and will He not make it good? Behold, I have received a command to bless; when He has blessed, then I cannot revoke it. He has not observed misfortune in Jacob; nor has He seen trouble in Israel; the Lord his God is with him, and the shout of a king is among them. God brings them out of Egypt, He is for them like the horns of the wild ox. For there is no omen against Jacob, Nor is there any divination against Israel; At the proper time it shall be said to Jacob and to Israel, what God has done! Behold, a people rises like a lioness, and as a lion it lifts itself; it will not lie down until it devours the prey, and drinks the blood of the slain* (Numbers 23:19-24).

After hearing that, any sane leader would call off the whole cursing thing and go home. Not Balak. He was a glutton for punishment, and probably kicked himself later for prolonging the torture (see Num. 23:27-30). Outlined plain and simple was the glorious future of the warrior people before him.

Still he begged the prophet, "Please stop. If you can't curse them, don't bless them." He had one more place in mind—to the wasteland perspective. There they went for the final showdown (see Num. 23:28).

But Balaam had found the connection. He had seen the light. He liked not being on the opposing team to God. An uncommon glory and favor covered the multitude and he dared not touch it except to speak of it. Abandoning his omens to conjure up the divine, he set his face upward and just breathed out the words as they came.

> *The oracle of him who hears the words of God, who sees the vision of the Almighty, falling down, yet having his eyes uncovered, how fair are your tents, O Jacob, your dwellings, O Israel! "Like valleys that stretch out, like gardens beside the river, like aloes planted by the Lord, like cedars beside the waters. Water will flow from his buckets, and his seed will be by many waters, and his king shall be higher than Agag, and his kingdom shall be exalted. God brings him out of Egypt, He is for him like the horns of the wild ox he will devour the nations, who are his adversaries, and will crush their bones in pieces, and shatter them with his arrows. He crouches, he lies down as a lion, and as a lion, who dares rouse him? Blessed is everyone who blesses you, and cursed is everyone who curses you"* (Numbers 24:4-9).

Wow! Beautiful and mighty, victorious and favored are the chosen of the Lord. These were the words that spun around in Balak's head as he listened to Balaam's prophecy. And they described the threat below him. These were not normal people. They were peculiar and singled out for something wonderful. Balak finally saw the writing on the wall. This people could be his undoing. It did not matter from which angle he positioned the prophet; his sights were set on cruise control to bless.

"Enough!" Balak's voice quivered with anger as he faced the prophet. "I brought you here to curse them, not bless them. Get away from me quick! You have no reward coming! Obviously, God does not want you to be rewarded either."

Balaam was officially fired!

Good thing, too. His final words were for Balak and his company. Balaam nonchalantly reiterated his initial position—he was not going to say anything that contradicted God (see Num. 24:13). That was not a secret, although Balak did wish Balaam had changed his mind. Balaam ended his defense by saying that he was staying on God's side, the side of blessing. No way was he switching even if Balak gave him his house *"full of silver and gold!"* (That sword in the angel's hand with his name on it was still vivid in his mind's eye.)

Preparing to saddle his donkey, the prophet paused and turned to Balak. "By the way, before I leave, let me tell you what these people are going to do to your people."

Without asking for the building of any more altars or sacrifices to be burned, Balaam set his face and let the words roll.

> *I see him, but not now; I behold him, but not near; a star shall come forth from Jacob, a scepter shall rise from Israel, and shall crush through the forehead of Moab, and tear down all the sons of Sheth. Edom shall be a possession, Seir, its enemies, also will be a possession, while Israel performs valiantly. One from Jacob shall have dominion, and will destroy the remnant from the city* (Numbers 24:17-19).

But that was not all. One by one, the prophet named off the future defeat and destruction of each nation there—Amalek, Kenite, Kain, and so on—except, of course, the Israelites. Certain that he was done, the prophet left. But the beauty of God's glory on a people was already painted and proclaimed.

So Balak grasped at a straw. Perhaps if Balaam could not reverse how God saw Israel, there were other ways to curse them. Maybe the Israelites could bring it on by their own doing. The Israelites' wrong responses to the curses could prove them guilty enough to invite in a curse. How cunning! He had to wait and see.

FROM UP HERE

In that sliver of time, Balaam got a glimpse of the God perspective. It took him awhile and some strong persuasions to turn him. But turn he did. He had to choose. That choice is not always packaged to our liking. It is always easier to look at life from where we stand. We don't have to do much. We just look and report. Finding God's view is more than just looking—it is more like stop, look, and listen to His heartbeat. Once we find the view of God on someone or something, the joy is definitely unspeakable. We do not budge easily.

We all look better from up there. God observes with an eternal perspective. Our temporal one pales in comparison. Or more like, it's a million miles off the mark. God's wonders stored into a human creation are something to behold and discover. Each one of us represents a unique trait of our creator. No wonder Paul declared:

> *Therefore judge nothing before the time, until the Lord comes, who will both bring to light the hidden things of darkness and reveal the counsels of the hearts. Then each one's praise will come from God* (1 Corinthians 4:5 NKJV).

People and things can change. Maybe not how or when we want them to change. Putting a clamp on our judgment is hard to do, but not impossible. Ever heard of an atheist, murderer, pervert, or satanist saved? How about our hard-hearted relative or our goody-two-shoes neighbor? It happens. Some of the most unlikely characters in our eyes have turned to follow the Lord with fervor. It is not up to us. That knowledge is sometimes hidden from sight. Taking a snapshot picture of anyone or anything in the now is easy. Sometimes the bad light they are seen in presents a juicy news report to revel in. Then here comes God—the One who never gives up on His handiwork or His investment. He has no desire to see anyone go down in flames, even when they deserve it.

Avenging ourselves on our enemy or someone that despises us seems satisfactory, especially if they have injured us deeply. Praying, "God, send fire on them until they get locked up or put in a hospital bed," is not God's view of blessing. His response might be more like, "No, I have to defend that. How about I put you in a hospital bed and they have such mercy on you that they'll come to you?" That does not sound like something we want to tangle with, either.

Praying something like this is the ticket: "I will bless _____ (fill in the blank). I will speak of the goodness of the Lord over them. It is the goodness of the Lord that brings them to repentance." That is a sweet shift from the vengeful attitude of cursing.

Considering God's perspective over someone or something is only a part of blessing. We want to become a willing participant. Try saying that out loud, even over your enemy. Ouch! It may initially burn our ears. Actually, that grinds at and kills the nature contrary to God's. I mean the one that imagines and cries for revenge. None of us likes a "thorn in the flesh," not even Paul, the great apostle who wrote most of the New Testament. "God, get me out of this!" We cry out to God as we see the "messenger of satan" edging in closer to harass us. In case we feel unfairly treated when this happens, Paul recounted for us a similar story.

> *I know a man in Christ who fourteen years ago—whether in the body I do not know, or out of the body I do not know, God knows—such a man was caught up to the third Heaven...and heard inexpressible words, which a man is not permitted to speak. On behalf of such a man I will boast; but on my own behalf I will not boast, except in regard to my weaknesses. For if I do wish to boast I will not be foolish, for I will be speaking the truth; but I refrain from this, so that no one will credit me with more than he sees in me or hears from me. Because of the surpassing greatness of the revelations, for this reason, to keep me from exalting myself, there was given me a thorn in the flesh, a messenger of Satan to torment me—to keep me from exalting myself! Concerning this I implored the Lord three times that it might leave me. And He has said to me, "My grace is sufficient for you, for power is perfected in weakness" (2 Corinthians 12:2-9).*

OK, that was not the answer we wanted to hear. How could a great man of God—caught up into the third Heaven, with prophetic insight, who knew the will of God and understood His mysteries—not get the messenger to stop? We can all surmise what this tormenting spirit might have been. He prayed three times but was told, *"My grace is sufficient for you."* God had given Paul all that he needed at the time, and then some more. Paul definitely had *"My grace,"* which means God's divine influence on the heart. I think the Lord was telling Paul, "You have inside you everything necessary to deal with this enemy; don't expect Me to come down and do the job for you."

We anxiously bombard Heaven: "Lord, I have this 'messenger of satan' working on me. Could You cause fire to come down and burn them? Let them know that You love me more than You love them? Deal with them. Wake them in the middle of the night and dangle them over hell. Oh yeah, and please hurry!"

God's reply might be closer to, "I have already put inside of you the power to bless and repel the cursing." Praying a blessing upon the person or situation sounds more like this: "Lord, let the joy of the Lord and the peace of God be upon them. Let them rest tonight and may they see the goodness of God upon their lives. I release the blessing of the Lord upon them." Our newfound peace makes room for the godly perspective and peace for our enemy. Blessing enthrones God to His rightful place where He can change people and situations.

God's available grace is not so we can "grin and bear it like a man (or woman)," as most of us have been taught. Nor is it for us to grit our teeth and say, "Bring it on!" Try blessing the environment and conditions of the situation and expect change. Radical, isn't it? God's power lies within us to bless and change the situation completely. Try seeing yourself as a thermostat and not a thermometer. Some people are great at reporting the temperature in the room and simply don't do anything to change it. You have the power to change the environment and set a peaceful temperature wherever you go. Blessing is God's thermostat that can affect the very atmosphere where you live.

I saw this firsthand while teaching on the power of blessing in a Bible school in Texas. A lady who was taking the course had told her friend about blessing the friend's boss. The friend quickly replied, "I am not going to bless him; I want to blast him." She called her boss various types of names, including "liar" and "cheat."

The lady who was in the class gave her a CD on blessing and told her to at least try it. She gave it to her on Tuesday; the friend reluctantly tried blessing on Wednesday and Thursday. She was the office manager, so she attempted setting the spiritual thermostat for the rest of the office. She recounted the sequence of events to her friend who had given her the CDs. She said, "On Friday, my boss called me into his office. The first thing I thought was, *I am going to be fired because he knows I have been in opposition to him, and barely do we even speak to one another.*"

To her amazement, he said, "I need to apologize to you. I have held you back from raises that were due you." He continued, "Starting retroactive from last month, you will receive your raise and promotion." She is now convinced that blessing releases God's favor and cursing puts everything on pause.

PRAYER

Holy Spirit, I ask that You help me to see from Your vantage point. Take me to the high place in the heavenlies and let me see as You see. What appears as rubble, You have declared, "This is what I want as potential!" God, help me not to back away from it. I don't want to spend the rest of my days trying to figure out why prophecy wasn't fulfilled. Help me to pass through what You want me to pass through. Open my eyes that I may have understanding of the hope that lies within me. Holy Spirit, help me to be aware of being a spiritual thermostat wherever I go. Amen.

Chapter Four

Power of the Tongue

It was a daily affair. Going by the topless nightclub in his neighborhood, the pastor cursed it.

"Dry up!" He spoke over that business to dry up and close up. He added, "And let no one come to your door," for good measure.

God was on his side. After all, did God not hate idolatry, fornication, and who knows what else went on in there? Feeling assured he was right on target, he went on his way for that day. Tomorrow, he would be back to do it all over again.

But there it was the next day. Customers were streaming in and out, and it looked like there were more patrons than the last time. It could not be! How could it be flourishing when God was dead against it? He would become stronger to the point of saying, "I curse you, unclean spirits; I command you to close these doors." It seemed the more he cursed the business, the more it flourished.

One day, while on his faithful tour to curse the nightclub, the Lord spoke deep inside his heart. The Lord asked him, "Why are you cursing the people that I have given My life for—the same life that I gave for you?" Then the pastor realized that the business was not the issue, but it was the blindness of those who patronized the place.

> *But I say to you, love your enemies, bless those who curse you, do*
> *good to those who hate you, and pray for those who spitefully use*
> *you and persecute you* (Matthew 5:44 NKJV).

Bless his enemies? What a concept! Blessing apparently was God's way of turning something from one way into another way. God was the "God of the turn and the return." This was new. But this was God's reply.

Like someone learning a new language, the pastor began to bless the owner of the club and the people inside. At first it was awkward, but he felt the pleasure of the Lord while blessing them. He realized that it was the goodness of the Lord that brings people to repentance. Within two weeks, the once-thriving club had shut their doors without any notice. Cursing causes darkness to thrive, and blessing turns things for righteousness sake.

What the pastor learned is a lesson that many Christians never seem to grasp. Blessing is an attribute of God. This took the weight off his shoulders—the burden of having to punish his foes. A new strategy for spiritual warfare was opened to him.

> *"May the Lord grant you all of His intention for you. I declare over*
> *you that God's full intention for your life from the beginning will*
> *come into fruition."*

God's plan for those who were caught up in frequenting that nightclub was not just for them to stop going but for them to find Him as a greater joy than the pleasures of sin. Many people can be convinced not to sin and still not find the place of enjoying their salvation from captivity.

This is our challenge. For this is where many of us have failed and fallen into condemnation. Our tongue—our vehicle for speech—has taken many of us down the wrong path. But it is the one thing that we need for the release of the blessing. Thinking blessing is only the beginning.

Speaking releases the blessing, and that calls our tongue into action. That also places a great responsibility on our tongue. We are literally prophesying or "breathing out" the breath of God (*pneumas*) as we bless.[1] Think about it. That is something not to be taken lightly. "Breathing out" blessing releases God's power to work in a person and situation. The words are there. The tongue waits. Soaking in eager anticipation of whatever thoughts we let loose, it wags them to life. How awesome it is when the words are those that breathe out the life of God!

> *Death and life are in the power of the tongue, and those who love it will eat its fruit* (Proverbs 18:21).

But not every tongue blesses. God had granted our tongue the power to wreak havoc or give life. Every day, our mouths exercise that privilege. When the tongue has done its part, the rest of the body has to deal with the consequences of those words—whether they were life-giving or not. We may unknowingly be feasting on the tongue's sweet fruit or rotten yields, because what we have is a power-packed appendage that is unruly. Add to that *"a restless evil and full of deadly poison,"* and we are left with a body part that needs to be controlled (see James 3:8). Honestly, no one wants something that powerful and toxic to be running loose. The tongue may be named as the culprit, but in actuality, it is an unrenewed mind or heart that feeds the tongue its content.

But no one can tame the tongue (see James 3:8). We have tried. What then? Bridle it. Yes, like the way we do a horse. A horse is a large animal that can be trained and directed by having control of the bits and bridle placed over the tongue and head of the horse (see James 3:3). James—a Son of Thunder, and a man whose sharp tongue earned him an unforgettable place in the Gospels—knew what he was talking about (see Luke 9:54). His tongue (and most of us can relate) was quick to condemn and bring judgment on any who disagreed with them at any given moment. James paints a vivid word picture for us to understand the power of the tongue.

> *Look at the ships also, though they are so great and are driven by strong winds, are still directed by a very small rudder wherever*

the inclination of the pilot desires. So also the tongue is a small part of the body, and yet it boasts of great things. See how great a forest is set aflame by such a small fire! (James 3:4-5)

Get the picture? This small appendage can set a direction and destiny just as a rudder directs a ship. But before we add more effort and energy to our task of controlling our tongue, here comes our help. God's Holy Spirit is our coach who teaches what to say. (See John 14:26.) He is about truth, the truth that pertains to Jesus, and He is our hope for a bridled tongue (see John 16:13). Bridling our tongue with a gentleness and vigilance beyond human ability, the Holy Spirit guides our tongues so it releases life more than death (see 1 Pet. 3:10). No thought or word escapes His patrol. Flagging the bad and releasing the good, words that bless begin to replace words that curse. Under His command, our tongue does not short-circuit our movement in the right direction.

In the long run, bridling our tongue under the power of the Holy Spirit has one outcome—Perfection. Definitely the direction we should be moving toward.

For we all stumble in many ways. If anyone does not stumble in what he says, he is a perfect man, able to bridle the whole body as well (James 3:2).

We are perfect if we do not stumble in what we say ("stumble" here means "offense"). Notice it does not mean stumbling at what others are saying. No matter what other people say, we can choose to keep our tongues under God's control. For a tongue under control means a body and emotions under control too. Now that is priceless.

Being seasoned in the things of God does not excuse us from keeping our tongues under the Holy Spirit's control. The prophet Isaiah recognized this truth. Bathed in the *shekinah* glory of God—the breathtaking and holy presence of the Lord—this seasoned prophet was only aware of one thing—the unacceptable condition of his mouth, especially for one who spoke for God.

Woe is me, for I am ruined! Because I am a man of unclean lips, and I live among a people of unclean lips; for my eyes have seen the King, the Lord of hosts (Isaiah 6:5).

This was his defining moment. Everything was in proper perspective in the light of the Lord's unspeakable majesty. He was a man sold out to God. His speech needed to reflect that commitment. Forget how he may stand out among the people—he wanted nothing else than to speak forth the will and love of the God whose splendor he was permitted to see. He cried out for God to deal with his unruly mouth. And God did—with a burning hot coal (see Isa. 6:7).

Maturity is more than just living long enough to know the consequences of our good or bad choices. Nor is it doing everything perfectly. Rather, it is allowing the Holy Spirit to direct our tongues in the way we need to go. Our words and lifestyle will reflect that inward movement. We learn to breathe out His words and life and abandon the desire to speak against our God-given destiny. No matter how big or small it may seem.

SEVENTY YEARS LATER

It looked impossible. The odds were against them. Rebuild the temple? Did God mean the rubble before them? Time had done its number on the remains of the temple. After 70 years of captivity, the ones that remembered the glory days of the temple were feeble in memory, sight, and strength (see Zech. 1:12-17). Returning home to rebuild the temple was a dream come true in itself, for the years in Babylon had only strengthened their longing for home. Zerubbabel and Zechariah, their leaders, surveyed the wreckage—definitely a God project. Rebuilding a temple out of the mess would take something more, something bigger than themselves.

'Not by might nor by power, but by My Spirit,' says the Lord of hosts (Zechariah 4:6).

Aha! So it was not about human intelligence or strength but, rather, about the Spirit of God leading and directing the job. That was reassuring. If the success of rebuilding the temple was determined by their dependence on God's Spirit, then it was wise to follow His direction. Suddenly, the insurmountable work did not appear as overwhelming as at first. It was doable.

Doesn't that sound just like God? Our impossibilities become places where, if we trust Him, we come to experience His grace and courage in surprising and pleasant ways. Then, like Zerubbabel and Zechariah, we can shout to our mountains:

> *What are you, O Great Mountain? Before Zerubbabel* [put your own name here] *you will become a plain; and he will bring forth the top stone with shouts of "Grace, grace to it!"* (Zechariah 4:7)

Remember our definition for "grace"—God's divine influence upon the heart. "May the Lord have His influence over you. May His intention for this pile of rubble come to its full potential."

For most of us, we spend more time reporting to God about the rubble. We have become experts in explaining the difficulty and gravity of the situation. Next time you face a pile of rubble, instead of reporting to God how big the problem is, try telling the problem how big God is. Now, that is grace that will move something!

Bombarding the mountain with shouts of "grace" was not the normal thing to do, but it was the God thing to do. Zerubbabel and Zechariah told that rubble what they were going to do to it—restore it into a glorious temple. This was potential. It was destiny. God's grace was evident in their elevated level of faith and in their speech. There was no room to complain, make excuses, or whine. Their words were an essential part of the rebuilding. Kicking over the rubble and going elsewhere to build was certainly an option. But Zerubbabel and the exiles never considered it or spoke of that. Rather, they embraced God's gift of grace as sufficient. Zerubbabel was responsible to keep them from despising the day of *"small beginnings"* (see Zech. 4:10 NLT). Nor did he quit. Possessing a finishing anointing (an anointing we need today), Zerubbabel and the exiles with him successfully rebuilt the temple. God's grace made the difference.

We have grace galore today. Grace is more than kindness; it's a gift. A grace invasion that fills our hearts spills out into every area of our lives. That includes businesses, relationships, and even personal decisions. Talking to our rubble then becomes no problem. We are confident and not intimidated by the situations we face. Grace keeps our hearts ever ready to repent should our lives and words become contrary or grievous to God. It is the God factor.

Looking at any "rubble" in your life lately? Not very pleasant, is it? The rubble represents an area in our lives that needs to be healed and rebuilt by the Lord. Naturally, we avoid it because it reminds us of our defeats, failures, and weaknesses—yes, all those things we want to ignore and wish away. Somehow, it keeps cropping up in our pathway. Though we try to pass it off on everyone else, God finally pulls the plug on us and we are left to face our mess.

"Have you tried speaking blessings to it?" God may ask.

Bridling the tongue remains a challenge, whether our destiny is as major as Zerubbabel's (or some other people we know) or not. Zerubbabel lived out the plan of God for his life and he did not speak against that destiny, nor did the people that were with him. They followed the prophetic word for their lives.

Knowing God's destiny for our lives does not mean that we will fulfill it. A personal prophecy does not come with a guarantee. It is the potentiality of God's heart for an individual. It is the proceeding word or the word that goes out in front. Prophecy acts like a catalyst that can start movement. It requires that we follow. It does not follow us. Think of it as God saying, "This is what I'm moving ahead in. If you'll follow Me, you can enter into a partnership that will be beyond what you could ask or think."

Prophecy is not a protection against death or a license to go our own way and do our own thing. People have told me that they cannot die because such and such a word was spoken over them and they have not seen it fulfilled. But I can attest to the number of funerals I've conducted of people with unfulfilled prophetic words. The Holy Spirit could not lead them. Some prophetic words will be fulfilled through and finalized in another generation, perhaps one of your children.

Following a prophetic word from God is no problem when we have a bridled tongue. But it's another story when our tongue is unbridled. We stand in danger of cursing our destiny, for our tongue can lead us down the wrong way and abort the word. Overlooking the conditions of a prophetic word is like forgetting to read the fine print. Regret is almost guaranteed.

WAITING AT THE RED LIGHT

Listening to the melodic voice of the water was soothing. A zebra sauntered over to join a pride of lions feeding on the grass nearby. Each was conscious of the other, but none was predator or prey—the curse had not fallen yet. Harmonizing to the whisper of the gentle breeze, the birds took to the sky as they greeted the sunlight with a song. The wind carried that song and the fresh scents of the land to the smooth seas. Alongside the river, a flock of sheep grazed as a pack of wolves ignored them as they made their way toward the sweet grass of the higher meadows. It was another perfect day. Adam smiled.

Suddenly, the Creator who watched this with pleasure announced to his attentive audience, *"It is not good for the man to be alone; I will make him a helper suitable for him"* (Gen. 2:18).

Huh? That was a first. His heavenly audience wondered in adoration. The DNA of the Creator pulsed with blessing. In His eyes, His every creation was good (see Gen. 1:4,12,18,21,25,31). He was pleased with all His work. Not one was an accident or a mistake. This time however, He found something that wasn't good—man being alone. And God created a solution—woman. Things were perfect.

Life did not continue in this bliss for long, however. Adam and Eve, the keepers of the garden, chose the seemingly good intentions of the serpent over God's plan for them. Everything that was good and perfect went awry, even the thoughts of humans. But God never changed His original plan. He intended for man to be a blesser.

Grasping the truth that God wants us to bless others does not come naturally. We like to pick and choose. After all, we reason, there are really wicked people who appear to need cursing. Aren't there? But didn't God form them in their mother's womb? Well, yes. Can we still say that they are sorry and no good? Why not say, then, "God, what You created was no good, and You made a mistake." No one wants to be spoken of as evil. James addressed that: *"With it (our tongue) we bless our Lord and Father, and with it we curse men, who have been made in the likeness of God"* (James 3:9). If that is not literally cursing God, I don't know what is.

With that revelation still fresh in my brain, I was driving in heavy traffic on I-30 in Dallas, Texas. It was a routine day when a small truck cut in front of me, almost clipping my car. Whatever his reason was, I was not sympathetic at all.

I blurted out loud, "You idiot!"

"What did you say?" That was my wife's voice in the seat next to me. That certainly was an unused word hidden away in my vocabulary bank, but nonetheless it surfaced.

As soon as I had said it, I heard the Lord deep inside of me say, "Why did you just curse Me?"

I replied again inside my heart, "Lord, You know I would never curse You," because I would be a crispy critter right now if I had.

I must admit I felt a little like Peter in the Bible telling Jesus, "You know I will never leave You. In fact, I will die for You." The Lord gently instructed me that everything created by Him has a purpose, and everyone has a part of Himself in them, even if they are an unbeliever. He told me to bless the young driver.

I retorted, "I don't even know him." The Lord persisted that I should bless him. Since this was my first attempt at blessing, I was somewhat clumsy. I started out by saying, "I bless you with everything God intends for you to have. I bless you with the knowledge of the Son of God, and you will get home safely so you can be a blessing to your family."

No sooner had I finished the blessing when I can honestly tell you I felt the pleasure of the Lord flood my body; it was as if the endorphins in my brain surged through me with ecstasy. I felt like the Lord was smiling on me, saying, "Now, that's My boy."

Place a blesser and a curser in a difficult spot and there is a stark difference between their responses. Worshiping God and blessing Him with song after being beaten and thrown in prison is the farthest thing from a curser's mind. The *"high praises of God"* are not in their mouth, and they may be wishing for a *"two-edged sword in their hands"* just to whack off a few ears. But not blessers like Paul and Silas (see Acts 16:22-34)! Their hearts and mouths were set to bless God no matter their situation. Though it seemed natural to accuse God of allowing them to go through hardship, they chose to sing. The Lord heard their music and He dealt with their oppressors. Their songs became the key to the prison doors and the opening for the jailer and his whole household to receive salvation. Wow! Paul and Silas could have missed that opportunity if they were busy whining and focusing on their troubles.

Even when a curser appears to be blessing, the motive for it might be way off the mark. Personal gain and comfort are generally in the forefront. When Jesus rode into Jerusalem on the donkey, those people shouting "Hosanna" were literally saying, "Come and take Your seat and rule Jerusalem." But God was not interested in Jesus kicking out the Roman occupation. Rather, the Roman conquerors were going to crucify Jesus. Ever before Jesus was the bigger purpose—the redemption of the whole world. And the only way to accomplish that was through His death. God wanted to rule in a higher place—the hearts of people. Not on some earthly throne! For when God captures our hearts, He has our mouths as well—successfully bridling our tongues—and He can control our entire beings.

So are you in a difficult situation now? Try singing, and imagine God saying to His angels, "That is my son (or daughter)! When they bless they are agreeing with Me." You never have to lift a finger to avenge yourself.

We cannot bless and curse at the same time. We are either doing one or the other. A spout cannot give out sweet and bitter water at the same time. Nor can our mouth bless and curse in the same breath. It is schizophrenic and double-minded to curse one moment and then bless the next. James tells us that anyone who does this should not expect to receive anything from the Lord. (See James 1:7-8.)

Recognizing that we may be cursing others is easier to do than realizing that we are cursing ourselves. Sometimes that is so subtle because we have become so accustomed to it. But our bodies respond to what comes out of our mouths. Seeing our bodies as a temple of the Holy Spirit is not always easy, especially when the mirror tells us that we do not measure up to the world's beauty and desirability standards (see 1 Cor. 6:19). Feeling harassed, being afflicted with physical pain, and getting old can be opportunities for us to speak blessing over our bodies. Saying, "I bless the hair on my head. I bless this heart, knees, and back because God's intention is not for me to be in pain," is like medicine over those ills.

Just as blessings come on us via our mouths, diseases and sicknesses may gain entry to our bodies the same way. So can detouring from God's natural design of blessing. I know of cases where crippling arthritis or ulcers have stemmed from bitter hearts habitually cursing everything that crossed their paths. Our tongues are meant to release the freedom and blessings of God on the earth. Forgiveness, accompanied with blessing the one you have just forgiven, seems to be more effective in releasing freedom to both parties. We can say we forgive someone, but when we bless them with a sincere heart as if Jesus was doing the blessing, the soul ties that bound us to the unforgiving spirit are broken. Many people have found freedom in their marriages and other relationships when they learned to bless in place of old methods of cursing and temper fits. We have the kind of marriage we bless or we have the kind of marriage we curse.

We can come to the place where the Holy Spirit is gaining control over our tongues, or rudders. This allows Him control of our ship—our whole being. We can begin to proclaim the solutions instead of rehearsing the problems. We begin to recognize the subtle forms of cursing in our lives, like giving up on something. Yes, we may not be using four-letter words of cussing, but by giving up on something, we are cursing it.

Jonah finding a ship going the way he wanted appeared to be the blessing of the Lord, but all the while, his destination was in the opposite direction, in Nineveh. What looks favorable to us may not be God's will or blessing. Blessing must be tied to the will and divine nature of God. In Jonah's case, he was able to sleep in the boat, because at the moment it seemed as if he was getting away with it. However, his escape in the opposite direction could not be God's favor on him, because it was in opposition to God's purpose for Jonah and Nineveh.

I dare to say that the reason some of us have not seen God's fullness in our lives is because we have not learned to bless what God has blessed. For the same reason, people become despondent and bemoan the fact that nothing good is happening to them. There obviously has not been any investment into blessing others. Blessing people with our mouths is an investment into our inherited blessing. We are promised that whatsoever we sow we will reap. Blessing is seed that we are given to sow that will affect both the recipient and the giver. Since we know that God loves a cheerful giver, we can conclude that He loves when we give blessing cheerfully.

PRAYER

Lord, I call upon You today. Please, bridle my tongue! Don't let my tongue be just in neutral so that I'm not cursing or saying any bad thing, but help me to be engaged to say good things. I want to be a mouth of blessing that You can train and direct in the way that I should go. Don't let my destiny be withheld because of an uncontrolled tongue.

I repent and ask You to forgive me for the times when I had an opportunity to bless, but instead I chose to curse. Lord, I want to bless everything You died for. Let me be a person that shouts "Grace!" instead of shouting the problem. Let me also be a person that has the gift of God in my mouth.

I pray that husbands and wives might bless each other physically, emotionally, and spiritually. Lord, I pray that I would bless everything that I come into contact with in my life. Wherever my foot treads, I pray that I would bless it and it would become blessed and holy ground, because when I bless You it becomes exclusively Yours.

I ask, Holy Spirit, that You put a guard over my mouth until it becomes like a rudder of a ship that You can turn in whatever direction You want, no matter how large it is. Let my tongue become a member of the Body of Christ. Let it be a tongue that is used to bless and is an instrument of righteousness. I pray that my tongue becomes an oracle that You can speak through, so that faith comes as others hear me blessing them. Help me to say what You are saying.

ENDNOTE

1. Biblesoft's New Exhaustive Strong's Numbers and Concordance with Expanded Greek-Hebrew Dictionary. CD-ROM. Biblesoft, Inc. and International Bible Translators, Inc., s.v. *pneumas* (NT 4151).

PART III

Activation of
BLESSING

CHAPTER FIVE

---❖---

MY BROTHER'S FAVOR

The long wait was over. Since the day he fled from his brother's wrath, he had assumed it would probably come. Now it was a day before the inevitable reunion—or would it be a fight? He did not know. Deceiving his brother seemed so great at the time and almost unforgivable now. How do you face your brother after you pretended to him, lied to your blind father, and stole what was meant to be your brother's by birth? Dread almost overpowered him. Jacob steadied himself as he saw his messengers return. They had gone on ahead to meet Esau and tell him of his coming. Maybe that was not a good idea after all.

The messengers reported, *"We came to your brother Esau, and furthermore he is coming to meet you, and four hundred men are with him"* (Gen. 32:6). Too late!

Jacob felt anxious. Four hundred men! That sounded like an army. Why, Esau could kill them all and take his possessions and his wives! He must not panic in front of his family and company. Courage—Jacob needed it badly. But 400 men! Esau must not be coming for a family reunion, but rather coming for revenge. That did it. Fear and distress came over Jacob and he hastily decided to split his people and goods up into separate groups.

He reasoned, *"If Esau comes to the one company and attacks it, then the company which is left will escape"* (Gen. 32:8). At least that was what he hoped.

Something was missing in Jacob's life, even though he seemed to have everything a man in his time could want—wives, children, servants, and animals (oxen, donkeys, and flocks) (see Gen. 32:5). He had run away with nothing, but now he was coming back home wealthy. The patterns of deception and fraud that marked Jacob were something he never really dwelt on or attempted to deal with. These patterns were evident, from the time he cheated Esau of the birthright blessing, to working 14 years to marry the woman he wanted, to the changing of his wages seven times!

Esau. Why, this deal with his brother hung like a boulder around his neck. How he wished it were all over! But Jacob knew that there was no way around this one. And from the way it looked, God was not providing any escapes either. He was not getting any younger, and running and striving were becoming wearisome. What he desperately wanted was favor. That's it. Not favor from God, for he knew he already had it, but favor with man, especially with his own brother (see Gen. 32:5).

Jacob was discovering a key to living life on earth—operating in the blessing is not independent of other people. To conduct business in a city, we need the favor of people. After all, when it comes to business and daily living, we deal with people. It is possible to have God's blessing and not that of others. That happened to be Jacob's case. The very thing that seemed to block him from fully receiving that favor was the issue with Esau. God intended for Jacob to eventually deal with the rift between him and his brother. God's interest was in victory over that issue, not in the cover up. Jacob was a man familiar with the blessing and favor of God. What he had yet to receive and experience was the favor of man. And it was time.

Writing off difficult human relationships is easy to do. But we are never quite free of them unless we confront whatever the issue was in the first place. God is always after the healing of those relationships. Fellowshiping with those that we have issues with is another matter. That is simply not a requirement. The joy of diffusing the power of shame that may arise from the broken relationship issue is worth the effort.

Receiving favor from others is a blessing. Even a marriage can be cursed if one of the spouses withholds blessing from the other (call that pure misery). Just because we say and believe, *"If God is for me, who can be against me"* (Rom. 8:31), does not mean that we are free of hindrances and opposition from others. This in no way means that we compromise God's will and Word in order to please people. What I am referring to is receiving the favor of people in order to accomplish God's will in a situation. We need both the favor of God and that of others. Even Jesus needed it: *"And Jesus increased in wisdom and stature, and in favor with God and men"* (Luke 2:52 NKJV). He was still a child then, and had a ways to travel before He got to His destiny—the Cross.

Although some of us can relate to Jacob and his need to find favor with man, there are times when we relate more to Esau. It is no secret that the enemy waits to assault us when we are in a vulnerable time or position, to steal our "birthright" or position of blessing. Those are the times when we are low in our faith, hurting, or susceptible to temptation—moments when we are too busy, too distracted, and too weak to care or pay attention. Yet some of us still falter to this strategy. Before we know it, we have been moved off the blessing and drawn into cursing. God becomes the enemy and the source of our pain, and we can begin to rage against Him. Evidently, our society manifests this position of anger and antichrist through anti-Semitism, banning prayer in school, pro-abortion legislation, and others like them.

WHAT IS YOUR NAME?

Jacob stood on the shore of Jabbok and watched his two wives, their maids, and his children swallowed up in the darkness (see Gen. 32:22-24). On the other side of the stream awaited his servants with all his possessions. Everything was in place for the meeting with Esau the next day. He was now left alone to face the weight of that deception so long ago. It was like another lifetime—but then again, it seemed only yesterday. Why?

In that desperate moment while Jacob prepared for his brother to arrive, he called on God. Wasn't it His idea that Jacob return home? Yes, Jacob realized that he did not deserve the goods that God had given him, but since this goodness came from Him anyway, deliverance from the "hand of Esau" would be great. Jacob was highly aware of his responsibilities as a family man and a businessman. More lives were at stake now. Running away was no longer easy.

For a moment, he quieted himself as he listened to the flowing of the Jabbok…until he saw the angel. In a few minutes, he discovered that this was the arena God had chosen for the wrestling match.

No, not physical wrestling. Can you imagine Jacob literally wrestling an angel? Why, with one flick of his finger, that angel could have thrown Jacob into outer space, and he could still be circling the globe! Rather, the wrestling was more of a debate. This word *wrestling* means "to come into debate over," or "wrestling with light." So, there stood Jacob on the banks of the *Jabbok* (meaning "poured out"), a river that emptied into Jordan and in turn emptied into the Dead Sea. He was ready to be "poured out."[1]

Jacob was distraught, but he was glad that God was listening. At least God understood his inner dilemma. If we could hear what the angel and Jacob were saying, would it be something like this?

Angel: "How about what you did to Esau?"

Jacob (sobbing): "I know what I did was wrong." Oh, he was truly sorry for what he had done! Finally, he was facing his own wickedness, the deceiving of his father and stealing what belonged to his brother. "But," he did not want God to overlook this point, "You covenanted with Abraham that You will bless those who bless You, and I, Jacob, have blessed You. Doesn't that count for something?"

Angel: "I blessed you, too."

Jacob (with a bit of a whiny voice): "Everything has worked out except this deal with Esau."

Pause for a moment. Have you ever been in such a wrestling? A wrestling of words can be just as energetic and demanding as physical wrestling. Does this sound familiar to anyone?

Husband: "Well you don't realize this happened today and I've worked hard and I've been bringing home the money."

Wife (irritated): "You don't know either…I've been home with the kids or I've been there for you all the time." (Don't even ask her to recite it, because she may have the list memorized!)

For Jacob, everything that went wrong in his life was someone else's fault. Esau was too careless and ungodly, too absorbed with hunting and his own stomach's comfort. His mother, Rebecca (bless her heart), conceived the whole plan for Jacob to get his blind father, Isaac, to bless him instead of Esau. (It was God's will for Jacob to have the birthright, but not through deception.) If he remembered correctly, he was afraid to do it, but she made him dress up in that fuzzy outfit and take Isaac that meal. Then there was Laban, his father-in-law and boss, a conniving and deceitful relative, to say the least. Come to think of it, innocence was something Jacob could not claim, either. Could it be that the reason the blessing of man's favor was withheld from him was his not taking responsibility for his life? The thought bothered him.

Come daybreak, the "man" was done but Jacob was still on the case. When it came to getting something he desperately wanted, Jacob was like a bulldog. He wanted the favor of God and that of his brother, and he was not letting go until he got it. Tenacity was a character trait that he had developed early in life. The angel knew that he would not let go until he had assurance of what was to come. Incidentally, he *"touched the socket of his thigh; so the socket of Jacob's thigh was dislocated"* (Gen. 32:25). Well, that was one way to end a nightlong wrestling match of sorts!

If only we were so determined to have God bless us. So determined that we would cry out; "Lord, against You and only You I have sinned. I have sinned and displeased You with my reactions and actions against other people. Please do something. I'm pouring out my soul and all my sin. My ways have not worked out. I'm not letting You go until I have this blessing, and the assurance that I'm going to be OK."

Then we hold on until we know that we have received it. Wouldn't that change some things?

Let's return to the wrestling match again.

Angel: "Let me go, for the dawn is breaking."

Jacob: "I will not let you go unless you bless me."

Angel: "What is your name?"

Jacob (*Didn't he already know?*): "Jacob."

This time it was more like a confession. He was "Jacob"—the "trickster, supplanter, and deceiver" or maybe even "tricky Jake." He was literally saying, "I confess; I'm a deceiver and a manipulator. I do certain things until I get my own way. I'm a pouter. I'm going to pout until I get my own way and make everyone feel rotten until someone gives in."

Finally, Jacob was willing to admit his faults.

Angel: *"Your name shall no longer be Jacob, but Israel; for you have striven with God and with men and have prevailed"* (Gen. 32:28).

God was declaring a new nature over Jacob's life, sealed by a new name. He needed a new nature, something that did not mark him negatively. Jacob got it. In that moment, Jacob received not only the blessing of God but also the blessing of man. Limping over to join his family the next morning, Jacob was a new man (see Gen. 32:27-32).

Morning brought more than relief to Jacob (er, I mean Israel)—it brought healing and restoration. Esau was running up to greet him with a hug and a kiss. Gone were the fears over this dreaded meeting. He had his brother's love and forgiveness. Jacob's new nature had taken hold, and he had no need to manipulate people anymore. And Esau, well, he could finally go on with his life. Jacob/Israel understood that his new name of prevailing was connected to his new nature of blessing—not only blessing God but blessing those He created in His image.

OUT IN THE OPEN

Eventually, many of us are like Jacob—we discover that operating in manipulation is not the way to obtain the blessing (hopefully before it's too late). Manipulation is a character of the enemy of our souls—even that of the "Jezebel spirit." Contrary to some popular belief, Jezebel is not a woman with red lipstick. Otherwise, we would have gotten rid of her long ago. The spirit of Jezebel functions through deception and manipulation, and in the Bible's account, it just happened to work through a woman (see 1 Kings 21:5-15). Manipulation is one person pulling on another. It is a symptom of not trusting God, but rather leaning on our own strength to get what we want. It is looking for someone to counsel us, say the right things over our lives, or give us the silver bullet to fix our situation. Yet we remain unchanged and nothing is fixed. Why? Solid within us may be the nature of Jacob that needs to be confronted and broken.

God is, in effect, speaking something like this over our lives: "I have declared over you for centuries that you are 'Israel.' Even from the beginning I have said that you are a man (or woman) of God. But you could not receive that, until you came to this place of confrontation where, instead of blaming others, you admit to the old nature."

A willing and repentant heart responds this way: "I am that man (or woman) who sinned. I messed up and no one twisted my arm to do it. It wasn't my parents, nor was it my children. I made a decision, and by doing so I withheld the blessing of God. Now I come to You today asking You to forgive me and set me free from having the same spirit as Jacob. I want the spirit of Israel as one who is prevailing with God and cooperates with Him."

The level that we are willing to deal with self is the level that we come into the blessing. Any "Jacob" tendencies in us only hinder the full blessing. Death to the "Jacob" nature starts by confession of our faults and letting go of our control over our own lives. Our eyes are finally opened to our own dead-end ways, and we become willing participants of God's good nature. We hear Him declare the new nature over us, and we are transformed. The hold of the old is gone and we are free.

MAN'S THREE BLESSINGS

God was pleased. From the seas and land to the animals and to humankind, He saw that His creation was good and perfect. So He added the final touch—the blessing.

> *God blessed them; and God said to them, "Be fruitful and multiply, and fill the earth, and subdue it; and rule over the fish of the sea and over the birds of the sky and over every living thing that moves on the earth"* (Genesis 1:28).

This was a crowning moment and the completion of His work. There was the creating and then there was the blessing. The blessing was not the creation, but what God said over it.

Three blessings were released over humankind in God's declaration. First, to be fruitful. That is the multiplication of humankind. The blessing of multiplication is for us to duplicate the life of Christ we carry inside of us. Second, to multiply and to cause growth. The idea is for us to be stewards over what has been given to us. I don't believe this is in reference to monetary status alone. We have a lot to oversee in how we conduct our life and its affect upon others. Third, to occupy and take dominion—to "take up space." As a believer in Christ, it means we are also to let the glory of Christ fill up those around us.

In one sense, we are called to have influence in the sphere of our contacts. This influence is multiplied through blessing.

The three blessings call us into proper relationship with other people—hence, our need for their favor. These relationships are vital to living and thriving on earth. This was something that Jacob eventually recognized. Isolation from society and poor relationships are rarely good for the healthy existence of a person.

To reproduce, enlarge, and prosper was God's intention for His creation. Here was a humungous universe and a beautiful earth. And just two people! More. God wanted increase. That is where blessing came in. Blessing blasts past the point of just surviving and getting by to a place of growth and aligning things to the purposes of God. It is zipping past the original point of birth to the point of exceeding fullness. From this one fish, God wants more fish until the ocean is teeming with its kind. Or from a marriage that is just surviving, God intends that relationship to be a great one so that it grows. These are believers having influence in a family, job, or community that goes way beyond simply surviving. For some, "normal" could mean being a wallflower without any risks. Blending in is not His intention. We need to cause something to grow and flourish, because there is something alive about us. Blessing brings about opportunities so we can show forth the goodness of our God.

Think about the man Daniel. He stepped out from just surviving into abundance. A queen recommended him to a heathen king to solve the mysterious writings on a wall:

> *...Because an extraordinary spirit, knowledge and insight, interpretation of dreams, explanation of enigmas and solving of difficult problems were found in this Daniel, whom the king named Belteshazzar* (Daniel 5:12).

What a reputation! Daniel left his mark in his world while living in a foreign, pagan culture. No matter his situation, Daniel stayed faithful to God and influenced a king and his kingdom. For that, God honored him highly even in a strange land. He was not complaining about serving a heathen king—he continued to prosper, influence, and live his life to affect the world around him. How? Daniel lived in the blessing and cooperated with God and had the favor of man.

WHEREVER THERE ARE WATERS

Ah, the blessing! Intended by God and released by human choice. Spoken over creation, it must be repeated and believed by the receivers of that blessing.

> *God blessed [barak] them; and God said to them, "Be fruitful and multiply…"* (Genesis 1:28).

We were meant to be carriers of the reservoir of blessing right from the beginning. When needed, a reservoir of blessing can supply the life ingredient that will cause something to grow and multiply. It is God's nature to bless, and thus it is in our spiritual DNA as well. When you find anything in your life that has become stagnant or unproductive, release the deposit of blessing that you carry.

All of us can learn how to bless. His Word is filled with prayers of blessing and words of life that can jump-start the deadest thing to life, whether it is a lifeless marriage or a rebellious child. We have received numerous accounts where parents have experienced incredible changes in their children by changing their ways from cursing their children with threats of failure to blessing them with the expectations of their future.

Abraham became such a reservoir for the families of the earth—a reservoir of blessing. His faith in God has affected generations for centuries. We have been adopted into the same family of faith through Jesus Christ. We have the same standing invitation that Abraham did. Even his descendant, Jacob, had to unblock what kept the pool of blessing from flowing.

God did not promise us a trickle of water. He not only indicated "pool," Jesus said "rivers." The Lord is always about over the top. Jesus promised *"rivers of living water"* that flow from one's *"innermost being"*—the same water that denotes blessing (see John 7:38). Those "rivers" are *potamos* in Greek,[2] and they speak of water that is not germ-infested (cursing), but rather, potable or suitable for consumption. Rivers that are suited for drinking are life-changing. David said, *"My cup overflows"* (Ps. 23:5). He was not referring to a tea cup, dainty and small, but the term actually meant a watering trough that allowed many to gather around and drink. His cup was always overflowing, never static and stale.

A reservoir has a continual outflow with an equivalent inflow. If we quit giving out, then we stop taking in. Proverbs says, *"A generous man will be prosperous, and he who waters will himself be watered"* (Proverbs 11:25). The simple truth is we are blessed because we bless. God takes no pleasure in seeing His children struggling to get by. And being born again does not mean that we have the pool of blessing flowing. Most believers are content to just have their needs met without recognizing that blessing increases their ability to help others. The Body of Christ has to move past believing God for needs and start walking in the richness and abundance of the Lord.

God does not respond to us from our neediness. He responds to faith. If you think all you need is a bigger need than someone else to get help, you will be disappointed. The Scripture says, *"...When the Son of Man comes, will He find faith on the earth?"* (Luke 18:8) He did not say, "Will He find neediness." Blessing is acting in faith by declaring what we know to be God's intention for the situation.

There are many families who live under financial and physical curses that hold them back from thriving. For some, they have grown up around the negative cursing where they blame others for their lack. They become accustomed to cursing their own family members, and so it perpetuates the generational continuum in their family. You can halt the forward progress of defeat in your family by breaking this cycle and starting to learn how to bless and not curse. You can break the cursing by advancing the blessing.

Rebuking the devourer proves to be a blockage to blessing. For example, we may be short-changing God, but we lose out when it comes to our money.

You are cursed with a curse, for you are robbing Me, the whole nation of you! (Malachi 3:9)

This was the instruction.

Bring the whole tithe into the storehouse, so that there may be food in My house, and test Me now in this (Malachi 3:10).

And this is the intended reward of obedience.

"If I will not open for you the windows of Heaven and pour out for you a blessing until it overflows. Then I will rebuke the devourer for you, so that it will not destroy the fruits of the ground; nor will your vine in the field cast its grapes," says the Lord of hosts. "All the nations will call you blessed, for you shall be a delightful land," says the Lord of hosts (Malachi 3:10-12).

Somehow, it is easier sometimes to overlook or explain this away. Tithing is always a test of the heart. Jesus talked more about money and giving than any single subject of His. It wasn't because He was looking to cash in, but it was a test to see if a person was ready to truly follow Him. Confessing much love for God and then withholding what He requires is inviting a curse on us. The withholding becomes an obstacle that hinders the intended blessing. There is no divine blessing without a heart that is obedient in honoring the Lord with our substance (see Prov. 3:9).

The windows of Heaven are ready to pour out on us, but it would be unjust for God to do so while we were negligent to His principle of blessing. God's blessings are always greater than our contribution, and it comes with a guarantee of Him rebuking the devourer. Now we can pay more than the light bill and keep the devil's paws off our stuff! In doing so we are representing the goodness of God to all we influence.

Favor sets us apart. Whether it is from God or people, favor is evident by the life one lives. Jacob's material riches, success, and protection were evidence of God's favor on his life. Reconciling with his brother was the beginning proof that he had been transformed from a deceiver to one who has prevailed with God through blessing. It only got better from there. Jacob's journey through life exhibited so much favor that his authority affected an entire generation and set a mark in history.

Israel was a name that reflected his new nature as a blesser. No longer would people see him as a conniving and deceiving man, but as a blessed man that they wanted to have around them. Our name can be of our own choosing—either that of a blesser or a curser. Life stages and circumstance are not always determining factors. God promises us a new name written in glory. It's on a white stone, and no one knows it except the One who wrote it. But someday we will know. What name will He write for you and for me? We choose.

It is our call. The ball is in our court. Are our fists clenched, and have we, in our pain, buried so deep the hindrances to walking fully in that God-intended blessing? It is time to reposition and confront whatever the hold may be. In the process, we may find some God surprises along the way. Ultimately, God's favor in our lives produces eternal confidence, but the favor of people makes it easier to accomplish God's will for us on earth. We need both. There is nothing better than to have the favor of the Lord resting on a life that is committed to being one who blesses.

PRAYER

Father, set us free from these religious cycles where we are fine for a while, until something happens and we blow up, feel bad about it, become ashamed and discouraged, and then feel better until we blow up again. Bring us to a place like You did with Jacob, where we break these cycles of "Jacobism." A place where we would no longer defraud one another, whether it is husband with wife, children with parents, parents with children, and so on. We do not want to rob You anymore.

Transform us to become a people of blessing. Fill us with blessing, as Proverbs says, "A faithful man will abound with blessing." Let us be so full of blessing that we don't have to think about it, but it just comes out of our mouths easily and we can say to others:

"May God's favor and blessing come upon you. May your full destiny come upon you! May your children love you and you love your children. May you be promoted and be blessed in the Kingdom of God and also here on this earth. May the God of all blessing overtake you! May you become fruitful, multiply, and occupy and say, 'Look! What the Lord has done!'"

We want to be able to say those kinds of things whether or not we believe them yet, just because You believe them. In that way, we are saying what You are saying and we are in agreement.

I pray over every family where there has been cursing. I break that cycle over them of cursing, divisiveness, and ill-speaking toward one another. Let Your Kingdom come let and Your will be done. May the power of Christ the Anointed One rise up inside us so that we even bless our bosses and those around us, and so we do not conform to the world's environment but create one through blessing.

Holy Spirit, let there be this wrestling inside of us to bring us to the person you want us to be. Thank You for the beginning of blessing. Loose us from poverty, sickness, unforgiveness, and from just getting by. Bring us to health and wholeness.

Endnotes

1. Biblesoft's New Exhaustive Strong's Numbers and Concordance with Expanded Greek-Hebrew Dictionary. CD-ROM. Biblesoft, Inc. and International Bible Translators, Inc. (5319). Wrestling means

to struggle with or debate. The reference to light was related to the angel in which he was struggling with over his deception. The Angel represented the light or truth. Also, Jabbok (OT 2999).

2. Strong's, *potamos* (4215).

Chapter Six

———✦———

Breaking the Silence

"I want to give you a promotion and a raise!"

She savored the words for a while, wondering if she was hearing correctly. Could this be a dream? Was this really her boss? The man who, for as long as she worked for him, had shown zero signs of wanting to promote her or give her a raise? Up to a few seconds ago, she had seen no course of action but to quit and end her miserable experience. Indeed, the turn of events could only be traced to a significant change she made a few days prior—the decision to bless the man she despised. And that had not been easy.

She recalled the conversation she had with a friend who urged her to bless her boss just two days before. Her friend had heard a message about blessing and eagerly shared it with her.

Well, she was not convinced. After listening to the message on the power of blessing, she decided to try it; she had nothing to lose. Since she was the office manager and used to getting there early, she began by praying for God's divine intentions to be released over her boss and the rest of the office. She repeated the same process on Thursday. The big surprise unfolded on Friday.

Her boss called her into his office.

Her first thought was that he was going to fire her, knowing they had been at an impasse for several months. He began by saying, "I need to apologize to you. I know I have been distant from you, and you deserve better." He continued on with, "I know you have been disappointed because you did not get the raise promised. Well, as of today, I am going to give you a raise retroactive from the time you should have gotten it along with a promotion." She was dumbfounded at the quick change that came by simply adjusting herself to bless and stop cursing him to anyone who would listen. God's original intentions, when appropriated, produce awesome results. She was not the only one. Take, for instance, a couple whose story I was privileged to witness.

They were choking up as they read the letter from their two teenagers. In that letter, there was healing, repentance, and joy. But it was not always like that. Just a week ago, this couple was beside themselves because their children were out of control and their family was on the verge of falling apart. These two children were rebellious and in trouble, pushing their home into a sort of war zone. It became them against us, and vice versa. What happened to the sweet babies they had raised?

Dragging themselves to another church meeting, they heard something different. This was a message of hope. They heard the message of the power that is blessing others. They grasped this truth with hope of getting their children back through blessing them! They knew the side of repeating how bad the children were and rehearsing their rebellion to counselors. Now it was time to try a different strategy. They were going to bless instead of curse. They began to replace angry words and expressions of disappointment with words of love and blessing—a difficult transition. Determined to walk this through, the parents hung in there and spoke blessings over their children. Then they saw it—the attitudes changed, the schoolwork improved, and peace came to their house. They knew the war was over. Blessing was here.

The children, too, became blessers. Scribbled on that piece of paper that day were their words of love for their father and mother, expressing their changed hearts. They acknowledged and were grateful for the love of their parents, their goodness, and their refusal to give up on them. The once-rebellious children had come home again. This was all in a matter of a week!

God's way is the best way, though sometimes it makes little or no sense at all in our minds. But it always spares us from needless grief.

JUST A SHADOW

No water. With the scorching sun on miles and miles of dry earth, every inch of moisture was sucked up, throwing just the heat in their faces. Today was especially brutal. Listening to the lowing and bleating of the thirsty animals and the murmuring of the masses for water was no way to continue a journey (see Exod. 17:1-7). Moses needed to do something. Egypt, the place they had just fled from, was increasingly becoming the Promised Land! Thirst and weariness skewed the multitude's thinking to the point where Egypt became the "the good old days," and that was voiced throughout the masses in mumbles and cries of "Egypt was much better." In reality, Egypt was never what it was cracked up to be. They had quickly forgotten the backbreaking labor and those slave drivers' whips!

God's instructions came to Moses at the right time. *"Strike the rock"* for water. Moses did, and a multitude's thirst was satisfied—until the next time.

They were in a dry place again and the Israelites were thirsty (see Num. 20:1-13). It was almost a repeat of the first story—thirsty masses, complaining people, divine instruction. This time, however, the Lord instructed Moses to *speak to the rock.* Moses still possessed the authority of God to hit the rock, but he was told to do something different. Spare the rod. This was a new season.

By now, the consistent complaining was getting to Moses. Understandably so, for not many leaders could do what Moses was doing—lead over two million people through hostile lands to a virtual unknown. With plenty of gripers and complainers in the mix who longed for Egypt, Moses was frustrated. He, too, was thirsty and tired. His sister Miriam had just died. Couldn't they see that? But they were too absorbed in their own circumstances to understand that God was leading Moses toward the promise.

Clearly alone in his own pain and frustration, Moses was at the boiling point. He was so focused on the complaints of the people that he lost the instructions of the Lord to only speak, not to strike. Moses' first words were to speak to the people instead of speaking to the rock. He raised his rod and called out to the people, "You rebels! Shall I bring water out of the rock for you?" Taking his rod, he struck the rock not once, but twice! Sweet, fresh water gushed out just like before. But for Moses, his journey to the Promised Land had come to an end. Now the promise could only be looked upon and enjoyed.

Cursing the rock came at a high price. The meeting at the rock the second time was to be prophetic demonstration of God's goodness. God wanted Moses to represent Him as the God of blessing who could be spoken to. God told Moses, "This happened because you did not believe Me, and so you did not honor Me before the people. Your unbelief is revealed." Cursing is a form of unbelief because if we really believed God and what He wanted to do, we would be blessing the rock (God's divine intentions).

Moses, like many of us do, became fixated on the circumstances to the point of losing sight of God's perspective on what is to come. Blessing is prophetic because it is able to see the way things should be, not the way they appear at the moment. Disobeying God, no matter the excuse, is not worth it. Not even when other people's actions or words bother us. Moses found this out too late. Yes, he heard God, but his annoyance at the people overcame him. The temptation to tune God out is there when we are mad at what other people are saying or doing. Yet, the specifics of God's instructions cannot be ignored. Producing results solely from our own strength and efforts diminishes and dishonors God. Cursing is, in a sense, smiting Jesus, the Rock.

Again, cursing is to place something in a lower position than God has intended. Those delivered out of Egypt may have been obnoxious at that moment, but God saw them as His chosen ones, not rebels. Speaking to the rock was a prophetic act representing the new covenant to come. Moses missed that part; he did not stop to think about the significance of his obedience at the time. That rock in the desert was a type of Christ. Present with them was the potential for water anytime they would bless or speak to the Rock, not just in times of crisis. Under the new covenant, Jesus the Rock abides inside of us. He is Christ in us, the hope of Glory. Therefore, when I bless you I am blessing the Christ in you—the One who can creatively turn things around and water the dry desert in you. We can say with confidence:

> *"Jesus, You are the Lord God who heals me. You are the God of my supply and salvation. You are the Jehovah Shalom. You are the Jehovah Jireh, the God of my provision."*

He is all those things and more. And as His name is, so shall His praises be.

WHAT WOULD YOU SAY?

"Moses says to stone her," declared the Pharisees. Seeing that this was an opportunity to find fault with Jesus, they asked Him, "What say You?"

The woman was caught in the act of adultery, and her punishment was already laid out, written by law—death by stoning (see John 8:1-11). They awaited Jesus' response, hoping to find an inconsistency in His teaching, expecting Him to say something against the Law of Moses.

This was Jesus, her Redeemer, the God of all creation in human form. Jesus was not going to surrender her to her accusers—those willing to curse her. Jesus turned the curse against her into freedom by blessing. Blessing is not a covering for sin, but a release from the curse of sin. It was easy for the religious leaders to report on this woman's life as if it would never change. They were willing to mark her as condemned. Jesus saw the potential in her life when she was freed from sin. In this case, the Blesser withstood the curser. Blessing always triumphs over cursing.

"He that is without sin cast the first stone." That was Jesus' reply.

Well, that hurt. He just called off their stoning party. Each one knew in his heart that he was not innocent. Slowly, they faded away, their own hearts condemning them. The woman was left alone before Jesus, still disheveled and stunned, but she was going to live! But she had been guilty, and she knew it. Jesus was still doodling in the dirt. What occupied the mind of this gracious Man? And what was He writing?

He straightened up only to ask where her accusers and cursers went. She knew they were gone, having heard the thuds of their abandoned rocks and the rustling of their robes in silent retreat. She replied, "I don't know, Lord."

"Neither do I condemn you; go and sin no more." And just like that, she was released from her sin.

What an obvious contrast between Jesus and the Pharisees! Each sowed something different into the adulteress' heart. The Pharisees sowed condemnation, while Jesus sowed forgiveness, hope, and life. Blessing does that. It deposits seeds of life into people's hearts and lives just as Jesus did. That seed of blessing has a blueprint that says, "Here is your destiny; walk in the fullness and purpose of God." Jesus broke the silence.

As always, God takes the initiative and breaks the silence to free a life that was written off by society. Then He gave us the same potential—the ability to break the silence. The Balaks of this life will always tell us to be quiet if we are not parroting their desires (see Num. 23:25). But that should not stop us from releasing the heart of God over people (see Num. 23:20). Though we may not find something to say in ourselves, the Word of God has plenty to say. God has lots of good things to say over people, and the Holy Spirit is always available to give us the words to speak when we don't have any.

Breaking silence is like plowing the ground. Words are like seeds that break the earth as they fall or are planted. If just talking does that, think about what praise and worship can do to hard dirt. Praise and worship breaks up the fallow ground of our hearts. Honoring God through our worship is the remedy for a heart or mouth that does not feel like blessing. It softens us. Seed is then sure to find some good ground. In the Garden of Eden, there were two significant trees that would have an impact on the future of all humankind. Most of us are familiar with the tree of the knowledge of good and evil. Adam and Eve were forbidden to eat from this tree, and from this tree the devil brought a seductive rational argument for eating. He appeals to the aesthetics and gets right to the point. "If you eat of this tree you will be as God." The rationality is that God is keeping something from you, and if you eat this fruit you will be independent from God because you will be like God. We know when they bit on that lie that they entered into a curse that caused them to take on the nature of the curser, the devil, and be driven from paradise.

The other tree was the tree of life. Adam and Eve were never forbidden to eat of this tree. In fact, they could eat of this tree daily. The tree of life was the tree of blessing. When they ate of this tree they were aware of God's goodness and His blessing, and they could have lived in paradise forever. When we curse what God has blessed, we find ourselves eating fruit that will drive us farther from the promises of God. However, when we bless, we are drawing from a tree that brings healing and prosperity to the soul. In turn, blessing brings us closer to the reality of our destiny.

> *Christ redeemed us from the curse of the Law, having become a curse for us for it is written, "Cursed is everyone who hangs on a tree"* (Galatians 3:13).

The seed of life that Jesus planted is incorruptible (see 1 Peter 1:22-23). It is the seed with a promise that came through Abraham.

> *Now to Abraham and his Seed were the promises made. He does not say, "And to seeds," as of many, but as of one, "And to your Seed," who is Christ. And this I say, that the law, which was four hundred and thirty years later, cannot annul the covenant that was confirmed before by God in Christ, that it should make the promise of no effect* (Galatians 3:16-17).

This seed of blessing we carry inside of us is DNA that cannot be corrupted. There is no iniquity in this seed. When blessing is sown into the heart of another, it causes the tree of life to take root and begins to crowd out the generational roots of cursing.

In that awesome exchange, we can now trade in death for life. Being *"crucified with Christ"* is laying down our fallen nature for His resurrected nature (see Gal. 2:20). *Part of being crucified with Christ is crucifying that part of our nature that curses what God has blessed.* Living out of the new nature of being a blesser elevates the life and anointing of Christ, which breaks the yokes of cursing over people captured by it.

THE PLACE TO BE

God has already spoken. When He speaks today, it is to confirm something that He had already said before. His Holy Spirit never contradicts His Word. He carries it out with precise cooperation, just like He did at creation. God spoke and His Spirit moved. Nothing materialized until God said it, which set in motion His Spirit to create matter out of nothing. God the Father spoke it and the Spirit did it.

> *The earth was formless and void, and darkness was over the surface of the deep, and the Spirit of God was moving over the surface of the waters. Then God said, "Let there be light"; and there was light* (Genesis 1:2-3).

The Spirit listened for the voice of the Father. God's voice moved His Spirit into action. A definite connection existed between the "saying will" and the movement of the Holy Spirit. The authority of the Holy Spirit is based on the Father and the Son, for they are One. This is the triune—the unity of the Trinity. This is divine agreement.

At the end of the age we can find another dynamic agreement in the Bride of Christ.

> *The Spirit and the Bride say, "Come." And let the one who hears*
> *say, "Come"* (Revelation 22:17).

Did you see that the Spirit and the Bride are both doing the speaking and not just meditating with good thoughts? Both partners are expressing the heart of the Father. God's "dynamic duo" of the Word and His Spirit execute the spoken blessings of the Lord. We get to join into this same union. When we bless what the Lord blesses, we are agreeing with the Spirit. When someone curses what God has blessed, they are in conflict with the Spirit and thus grieving the Spirit of Truth. People who are given to cursing are more likely to be deceived than blessers. Those who are submitted to blessing are in unity with the Truth.

> *If you abide in Me, and My words **abide** in you, ask whatever*
> *you wish, and it will be done for you* (John 15:7).

To *abide* in us means to literally "pitch" His tent. God's Word wants to camp out in our lives. He is not just going to be our neighbor, but He is moving in and taking over. When we pitch our tent in His Word, He will pitch His tent in our hearts. The Holy Spirit takes the *logos* (the said word of God) and turns them into the *rhema* (the revealed word of God or the saying word of God) and it becomes revelation. God's words are spirit fabric or substance (see John 6:63). They have a life of their own, and they are powerful enough to transform minds with the life of God.[1]

Camping out with God in His Word is a position of blessing. He couldn't have made it any easier to find His heart and will. His words take hold of our hearts, and by faith we speak them out.

When we use the Word of God to declare blessing over a person or situation—just as the Spirit brooded (literally, "to inseminate") over the waters at creation—the Spirit is released to work according to the blessing of the Lord.[2] If you know of someone bound by drugs, you can bless them by declaring God's intentions over them as opposed to those who simply reminded them of how wretched they are. Blessing does not focus on what is happening at the moment, but is intent on what God originally intended. Cursing causes one to get off on a detour in life. Blessing rehearses the highway God intended them to take.

Undoubtedly, this is a radical shift for some who are used to sitting in the seat of the scornful. An unlocking of God's creative word via our mouths occurs from the seat of those who bless and curse not, as Jesus admonished.

Definitely, we don't need a "saying word" without the moving of the Spirit, for frustration is the end result. But there is a moving of the Spirit of God when blessing is the motive of the heart. Without the Holy Spirit illuminating the Word of God, the word becomes a dead letter.

To believe God's Word and that He is who He says He is pleases Him. That happened to the centurion in Matthew (see Matt. 8:1-13).

Centurion: "My servant is home, sick even unto death."

Jesus: "I'll go and heal him."

Centurion: "No, I'm not worthy for you to come into my house." The centurion had faith that Jesus' words had power and authority even to the point of Jesus just speaking the word of life. "Just say the word and my servant will be healed."

Jesus: "In all Israel I have never seen such faith."

Jesus was highly impressed with this Roman soldier, who was not a Jew nor schooled in the Scripture. The one thing this soldier understood was authority. He recognized Jesus had authority that was beyond just the normal teachers in Jerusalem. His authority had power that brought about changes in the lives He touched with His words.

The power that is in blessing has authority to change the balance of circumstances in the favor of the blesser. Just send the word of blessing that is the will of God for everything He created. God declared everything He created in Genesis was good. Opposing what God has called good brings us into conflict with Him.

A DEEP, SMILING PEACE

Immeasurable, unspeakable strength is the joy of the Lord. This is the intangible side of blessing and evidence of the divine seed within us. A peaceful home and loving family relationships are blessings that cannot be measured like material wealth. Yet it is still one of the riches of the Lord. The family we met at the beginning of this chapter experienced it.

> *Blessed be the God and Father of our Lord Jesus Christ, who has blessed us with **every spiritual blessing** in the heavenly places in Christ* (Ephesians 1:3).

Joy comes with the Holy Spirit and is a spiritual blessing. Like deep waters, it only needs to be drawn out and allowed to spring up.

True joy cannot be hidden. If it is there, it will show up whether we are trying or not. It radiates on our countenance, and it lingers on those we come in contact with. With material possessions we can blend in with the crowd if we want, but we wear joy. Joy knows no bounds, for it crosses all circumstances and the settings do not limit or restrict it. Nor does it discriminate on social or economic status, age, ethnicity, or gender. The carrier of the joy is who matters. Sometimes it shows up in the oddest places. Joy is a believer's mark and evidence of God's Kingdom. It is also our strength that signifies separation from the world. Watch the faces of those in the world and read the message—agony and depression. Does anyone have life and hope? Here comes the "church," the "called-out ones," and the world is searching our faces. Are we any different? Or do we, too, carry the strain of the agony and depression that the world carries?

The presence of joy on our lives simply means that we have accepted God's loving-kindness as a fact of our life. Joy exhibited is blessing released. This is the open door for people to see God's good intentions and purposes for us. Otherwise, they have nothing to hope for.

Joy is different from happiness. Happiness is based solely on happenings. If we had good news for the day, that causes us to be happy. It is possible for one to get bad news and still keep joy. Joy is eternal and happiness is fleeting at best. Joy is an attribute of the nature of God. This is why it is described as the joy *of* the Lord, not the joy *for* the Lord. The lifestyle of blessing keeps a fresh download of joy continually pouring into the soul.

We have been made an offer that we must not pass up. One who learns to bless and bless often exchanges a life of resistance for one of favor. If you are facing something as hard as stone and it appears hopeless whatever you do, then before you give up try this. Daily speak to the situation with the Word of God, knowing your loving Father in Heaven wants an outcome that glorifies Him. Failure is not the outcome God would choose. Blessing is like water dripping daily on the stone until it gives way to the will of God. Everything you need to live a life of blessing is available to you: the Holy Spirit, the Word of God (living and written), an incorruptible seed with creative DNA, and a God that backs up His promises. Once you taste the benefits of blessing, no one can convince you otherwise. Just ask the woman who got a promotion or the couple who now have a peaceful home.

BLESSING

I bless you today, by the heart and power of the Holy Spirit. I release upon you God's goodness and favor. I release upon you the oil of joy. I release upon you the presence of God, so that from the wells of salvation you will draw water for your thirst in life. May the Father's good pleasure be upon you, for He delights in and desires you.

Old things have passed away. Begin to walk in the newness of life and the revelation of what shall be because of the future and hope that lie before you. God has delivered you from your enemies and has opened for you the door of salvation. You have the key of David that opens and that no one can shut. You will walk in the fullness and prosperity of God. Even as your soul prospers, so shall your spirit be quickened and made alive according to the will and purposes of God.

May your children be taught of the Lord and may His fullness be upon them. No weapon formed against you shall prosper, for this is your heritage as a child of God. May you eat to fullness; the enemy shall not steal bread from you, but a table shall be prepared for you in their midst. No longer shall you have bags with holes in them, for the honor of the Lord is to release upon you His expectations.

Walk in the power of the Holy Spirit so that you will not fulfill the lust of the flesh nor be bound by the fear of failure. For the Lord declares over you that you are victor and not a victim. His intention is that you show forth His loving-kindness and His mercy and that you walk in the full dimension of the Holy Spirit. You will not diminish, weaken, depress, or grieve the Holy Spirit of promise, but you will allow Him to be fully who He is to be.

ENDNOTES

1. Biblesoft's New Exhaustive Strong's Numbers and Concordance with Expanded Greek-Hebrew Dictionary. CD-ROM. Biblesoft, Inc. and International Bible Translators, Inc. (3306), *logos* (3056), *rhema* (4487). Wrestling means to struggle with or debate. The reference to light was related to the angel in which he was struggling with over his deception. The Angel represented the light or truth. Also, Jabbok (OT 2999).

2. Strong's 7363.

CHAPTER SEVEN

SUGAR WITH YOUR COFFEE?

He looked familiar. Assured that he had visited our church in the past, I abandoned my spot at the Starbucks line and went over to say hello.

"Hey, how are you doing?"

His eyes narrowed with an unpleasant recognition. But I could have been imagining.

"Get away from me!" He was abrupt.

This must be a joke, I thought. So I kept on walking toward him.

"Get away from me! Get away from me!" Now he was adamant.

Whatever his beef was with me, I was clueless. But I decided to play the game. I edged closer. That only agitated him further so that he was gesturing madly at me to "keep my distance." Clearly, he did not want me to close the gap. I stopped.

"Get away from me! I bind you...!" *Huh?* I was floored. "You are a sepulcher full of dry man's bones! You religious thing, get out of here!"

Taking that last cue, I retreated. But I was completely caught off guard.

Recounting the whole story to my wife later was difficult. I had never felt so slammed in my life. Completely hurt and sickened by the incident, it was all I would talk about for days. What had I done to the guy to make him so angry? Praying for him and asking the Lord for forgiveness for offending the man in any way did not lift the incident off my mind. It hung on stubbornly.

Until, one day.

Why, the Lord asked me, did I hold on to the bad things longer than I held on to the blessing? That got my attention. Then, He proceeded to set my mind free from the Starbucks episode.

They Come Knocking

Why does it take more compliments to counteract one negative thought? And why do we instinctively have a propensity toward the negative? It does not seem to take much to foil a wonderful day. Closing time approaches and you are flying high. The boss had complimented you, and everything had gone smoothly at work that day. Suddenly, someone comes and says or does something negative to you and ruins your whole day. Whatever they did and said bothers you for hours or maybe days. Consequently, you end up in frenzy because one person was negative toward you. But wait! You forgot that ten people complimented you that same day!

Essentially, we empower whatever we set our hearts to meditate on. To ponder God's Word is to give it power in our lives. But lying awake at night, tossing around in our minds what people said or did empowers the curse. Each time we chew on the negative too long, we move closer to the side of the curser. That makes us more vulnerable to agreement with a spirit that opposes the nature of God. Inadvertently, such an agreement (whether we are aware of it or not) would bring an inheritance of the not-so-pleasant kind.

Accepting an accusation and receiving it into our spirit is letting go of what God has said. By grabbing the lie, we lose our hold on the truth. We easily shrug off words like these: "God's hand is on your life and He has good things in store for you. He wants to do great things in the Kingdom through you." To us, they become something nice that someone is supposed to say, even though they are true. It is difficult to keep our grip on what is true if we are embracing a curse.

Even in situations where we hear of other people's difficulties and pain, our reactions do matter. Actually, our reactions are a good indicator of whether we understand the heart of God when it comes to other people. Do we reject the desire to gloat over their hard time (especially if they had hurt us), or do we happily say or think, "I knew it! I knew it! They messed with me and God got them." This is hardly the heart of God. Nor is it the heart of a very good father. Does God love me more than He loves them? If so, is He avenging me? No, Jesus came to deliver us from the curse, not add to it.

Choosing life or death is an ongoing process. We have to sift through the myriad of actions, situations, thoughts, and words that come at us daily. We can either take it or leave it. But they are not always obvious, arriving with a label or announced. Because we know that even if our friend offers us poison, and says, "I am your friend, drink this poison. You don't love me if you don't drink this poison," we would have no problem saying, "No." Yet the deadly poison that would ensnare us with a destructive agreement may be subtle in its presentation, but packaged in the power of suggestion and superstitions.

Avenues that spread the fear of diseases are numerous today, and we continually have to resist their onset. Never underestimate the power of words, even from seemingly innocent remarks. Thoughts that promote fear of the unknown are toxic and should not be given any time or space on our mental "to-do list." Proverbs 23:7 tells us, *As he* [a man] *thinks in his heart, so is he.*

God is all about creating life and recreating Himself inside our minds so we can have the mind of Christ. Choosing life provides us with the ability to continually repeat the things that duplicate or multiply the life of His Spirit. If something does not speak life into our spirit then we don't have to receive it, even if it is from our best friend!

THE HEARING EXPERIENCE

Another mealtime and another restaurant, but this is one you have never been to before. When handed the menu, your eyes glance over the list, linger, and skip over to find something familiar. You are slightly stumped. What to eat? Suddenly, the waiter comes by with his pen and notepad and you realize that you are not ready to order. You need some help with the selections.

You ask, "Is there something here that you would recommend?"

He points to an entrée. "This is a real popular item and I've eaten this. It is great! I recommend it."

"You've eaten it?"

"Yes, I've eaten everything here on the menu. I can recommend it; you won't go wrong." He seems believable so you order it.

It would be a different story if he replied, "No, I won't eat here. Just pick anything. It is all the same." At that point, you either leave or stay and form your own opinion. But then, the weight of an employee's recommendation is considerable.

People who recommend something do it because they have encountered that thing and their taste is set for it.

I understood this in a very real way many years ago while speaking at a conference in Cuernavaca, Mexico. It was a large gathering of several hundred people from various churches all over Mexico. When I arrived, I was escorted by trained ushers to the front seat. Directly in front of me were three giant speakers piled one upon another. While waiting for the service to begin, I did not really think about where I was positioned. When the worship team hit the first chord, I understood the concept of Encounter. I ceased hearing and began to encounter the vibrations going through my body. I remember the encounter of that moment more than anything that was sung.

How we hear God is an important aspect to receiving blessing. The Holy Spirit is constantly speaking to us about blessing (see Mark 4:3-9). Take, for instance, the parables that Jesus spoke. To the outsiders, the stories of Jesus were just that—stories. The meaning and truth were hidden from them. Understanding the truth was their ticket to true freedom. But although they were all ears, they were not getting it (see Mark 4:10-12). He really does want us to know the mysteries of the Kingdom of God. The word *mystery* simply means it cannot be discovered by a casual glance. It is translated, in my words, as "that which cannot be seen through natural understanding." Having an encounter in the presence of the Lord causes one to see the mysteries from the perspective of Christ, and then they are no longer mysteries. These mysteries enable one to bless when the circumstances may cause one to want to curse the situation.

Unbelief and suspicion can do that, too. Have you ever received something from someone and your first thought is, "I wonder what they want from me"? People who have trouble trusting due to broken promises and perhaps being defrauded in some form will have difficulty receiving blessing bestowed upon them. God does not disappoint. Disappointment comes from a preconceived idea that was never God's anyway. God is all about appointments, not disappointments. Blessing is filled with His intentions for your life that are backed up by His written Word, but it is released as a catalyst when it is spoken or prayed over someone.

Rejecting the blessing is not the only challenge. Temporarily receiving the blessing and then discounting its power and letting it go is another.

Believers can also take the holy things of God (like a prophetic word) and cast them before people who are oblivious to the value. It is not a pretty sight when the swine trample the things of God underfoot. We lose out on the blessing because someone who despised prophecy was more familiar with cursing than the power in blessing.

They should not be surprised if they find themselves stuck in the same condition years later. Yet, we were given a catalyst from God to get us unstuck and bring us into a fuller life of joy and abundance. Backing away from that word of blessing results in the maddening cycles just being repeated again and again. We need to contend for the blessing. Although it seems easier to believe the lie than the truth, both require a similar action—belief in something bigger than us. If the lie or curse is given life by believing in it then it becomes bigger than we are, and before long it has taken the position of power to the point of consuming our thoughts and devouring our hopes.

So where will the seed of the Word land in our life? On the roadside where it is exposed to the birds of skepticism? Where the sun can scorch and burn out any joy of life? Choked out by the cares of life? It does not have to be that way. It can land in our hearts in the fertile ground of faith. We can become skillful in handling the genuine truth through blessing, and this will keep us from being deceived by curses.

THE RECEPTION

In an instant, everything had changed. He had been frustrated and enraged. The other car was not driving fast enough in the left lane to suit him. Nonetheless, they were not letting him pass, nor were they trying to switch to the slower lane. Agitated by this time, the man rammed the family's vehicle. The car flipped into the face of oncoming traffic. Moments later, he learned that every single person in the vehicle was killed. His uncontrolled anger had now turned tragic and destructive. His road rage had turned what was to be a time of holiday festivities into a nightmare.

The way of the cursers never finds favor, no matter how much they justify their reasons for their actions. For that man, his assumption that someone was obstructing his way resulted in violent deaths. His anger stemmed from a life of cursing, and the road rage was simply another step in its progression. It cost him his inheritance and any blessing that was available to him. Had he been a blesser, the outcome could have been very different. Cursing in some cases is a matter of life and death physically; in other cases it is a matter of life and death of the soul.

Ponder for a moment the parable of the prodigal son and his elder brother. Although the elder brother faithfully served at home, he was resentful of his wayward brother. He was also resentful of the unearned love that his father had for this prodigal son. He had great difficulty when his brother came to his senses and was restored to favorable status and treated to a homecoming party (see Luke 15:11-31). On the same day, he was dumbfounded to learn from his father that he could have had a party the whole time. He could have been celebrating with his friends continually. He was not able to enjoy his inheritance due to the anger and injustice he felt toward his brother. His cursing kept him from a relationship with his father. Instead, he settled for only a working relationship. He never discovered the intimacy he could have enjoyed with his father. His heart was poles apart from his father's. His nature was more familiar with cursing and judging only the circumstances, whereas his father's heart was inclined toward blessing. Since the father had a blessing heart, he was able to see by faith into the future and his son's return. The elder son had never understood his father's desire to bless his brother.

Our inheritance may be on hold because we don't see with eyes of blessing like our Heavenly Father does. The principle of sowing and reaping definitely fits here. When we curse by speaking against the mercy and will of God the Father, we are blinded from seeing our portion of the inheritance.

Those who bless see things in the opposite spirit from that of the world system, which is more inclined to curse anyone who is not as miserable as they are. God's Kingdom is relevant for today. Though we are in this world, we are not part of its system. The Kingdom of God is a Kingdom pronouncing good news. This world system, however, is pronouncing captivity through the culture of cursing. This way of life is filled with anger and a lot of mistrust. People who are aligned with cursing are more apt to deceive without remorse, because cursing hardens the heart to the point of callusing the conscience.

In the Gospel of John this conflict of culture is confronted.

*From the days of John the Baptist until now the Kingdom of Heaven suffers violence, and **violent** men take it by force* (Matthew 11:12).

We usually think of violence as something that is militant and angry. Violent—*biadzo*—is translated "to crowd out."[1] The idea is that when something fills up the space, it crowds out what was there before. For example, a glass filled with water pushes out any dirt that happens to occupy the glass. When Jesus comes into our life, He will crowd out those things that are in opposition to His nature. The prescription for breaking a life of cursing is to be filled with the Holy Spirit who will speak from the nature of Christ.

The fruits of the Spirit are love, joy, peace, patience, kindness, goodness, faithfulness, gentleness, and self-control (see Gal. 5:22-23). These are attributes of blessing. It is interesting that they are referred to as the fruit of the Spirit. These qualities are developed in those who are willing to bless. Blessing doesn't leave any room for the dark side of cursing. The art of blessing has a way of crowding out what does not belong. Cursing gets crowded out and finds no room to launch from.

Love and mercy, by contrast, are characteristic of His Kingdom. They crowd out anger and false judgments. The culture of blessing and the culture of cursing are always at war. Blessing leads to faith and the pleasure of the Lord, whereas the culture of cursing leads to unbelief and condemnation. Ephesians tells us to put on the new self which is created in the likeness of God. Laying aside falsehood (cursing), speak truth (blessing) to one another. Don't give place (opportunity) to the devil. (See Ephesians 4:25-28.)

The devil looks for opportunities to corrupt and pollute what God has blessed through cursing. Many times when this happens to us, we fire back our missiles and before we know it we have fought cursing with more cursing. We leave there feeling condemned. The only way to win this war is not to return evil for evil, but instead give a blessing. Nothing disarms cursing more than giving of a blessing in return. Blessing always trumps cursing. Jesus said, in

Luke 6:28, *"Bless those who curse you, pray for those who mistreat you."* There we have it—the strategy for overcoming the devil. The devil tries to bait us to fight evil with evil. Jesus says the victory is in the blessing. Remember, blessing is pronouncing God's intended favor upon them, not what they deserve. Blessed are the merciful; they shall receive mercy. Blessing and mercy are partners, and when we sow them we reap the favor they bring. I don't know anyone that does not need more favor or mercy.

Speaking blessing is giving agreement to what God sees as the potential in a life. At the same time we give that agreement, the enemy tries to steal our faith in God's Word by painting a different picture of our destiny. Whether attractive or dismal, we are not to believe the enemy's alternate headlines of the day. God's Spirit will *"lift up a standard"* against the enemy (see Isa. 59:19 NKJV). Most people refer to this verse as, *"When the enemy comes in like a flood, the Spirit of the Lord will lift up a standard against him."* However, the original intent was translated to read, *"When the enemy comes in, like a flood the Spirit of the Lord will lift up a standard against him."* The comma is like the blessing—when we bless we change the intent from the enemy being as strong as a flood to the Lord being the flood that defends us in conquest.

The standard was a flag to show the fight is still going. I think the standard we wave is blessing, and it turns the tide of a battle to victory. The way the devil gets us defeated is to pull us to his side of agreement, as in the case with Balak and Balaam (see the story in Chapter Three). The devil may not be the only challenge to receiving blessing. Growing up in an environment where blessing was not handed out by a parent or guardian may seem to be awkward. Therefore, if people rail at us we readily defend ourselves with equal volleys of the same. Fortunately, we have the opportunity to change our tactics and expectations by cultivating a grateful heart that gives blessing in spite of cursing.

Those who learn to bless skillfully will get to their desired destiny much quicker. Those who think their strength lies in their toughness of heart and mind to beat someone down with words are farther from God's plan than they know. Blessing is one way we show that we truly trust God, because we leave the outcome to Him. Cursing may feel good at the moment to the low end of our flesh, but the end result is that we have fallen into the same pit as our enemy. The devil's playbook contains the plan to get you to look at areas of unfulfilled desires and accuse God of being unfaithful to you. Does that sound absurd? Well, consider this—complaining is one form of saying, "God, You have not done a very good job of taking care of me because of blah blah blah." Complaining was the main thing that angered God the most with the children of Israel while in the wilderness. Rejecting blessing is to reject God's prophetic input in our lives. Have you noticed that sometimes when you try to bless someone, they do the unworthy thing?

Some are so beaten down that any blessing placed on them will seem foreign. But we are to keep blessing, allowing the Spirit to work and break through the shield of death around them. Once they are free, they will become a strong proponent of blessing. God pronounced blessing on Abraham so he could become a blessing to all the families of the earth. God said:

> *I will bless those who bless you, and the one who curses you I will curse and in you all the families of the earth will be blessed* (Genesis 12:3).

God introduced blessing into the earth through a man. He blesses one so they can in turn bless others. Blessing is generationally contagious. When a family starts a practice of blessing, it causes a reaction that will affect their entire home. It flows from the head of the house down to everyone else and out to the teachers through the children and on to their friends. Blessing cannot be stopped.

Abraham became a blessing to all families, because when God blessed him he received it. If Abraham had not received the blessing, then he would not have been able to be a father of many nations. In that case, Jacob would not have been around to lay hands on his sons and declare God's intention for future generations.

Any declaration of God over our lives requires a response. This is essential in receiving blessing. It's worth noting Mary's response to the angel announcing her immaculate conception. She said, "I don't know how this could be true, since I have not been with a man, but nonetheless, *'let it be unto me according to your word.'*" She could not understand the logistics of how it could happen because it was out of the ordinary for sure. However, she still accepted the declaration over her life as the blessing of the Lord. Her response was one of a humble and willing heart. Yet I hear people say, when they received a prophetic word, that they put it on the shelf. Nowhere does Scripture speak of a shelf for putting prophetic words. If it is not God, why do you need to clutter your shelves up with it?

Just receive the word of blessing and leave the rest to the Holy Spirit. Prophetic words that give life are to be believed, embraced, and watered by prayer. Mary, the mother of Jesus, did this (see Luke 1:38). Instead of trying to figure it out, Mary simply agreed with God. Believing and receiving the word of the Lord leaves no room for the enemy to play mind games as he did with Adam and Eve in the Garden. He does so by asking us the question, "Did God really say…?" When we believe God, our hearts are tender toward Him and we are good ground, ready for the seed of life. Instead of rehearsing threats or consequences, why not bless them with the potential of God's favor. The old adage is true: "You can catch more flies with honey than vinegar." Some have used vinegar for years because they grew up on vinegar. Jesus wants us to get a taste of honey so we won't go back to vinegar. Why not try something like this?

> *"God intends that you become successful and be a man or woman of God. You are going to rise up and call Him blessed. All the days of your life will be filled with great joy. Many will be blessed because of you."*

Imagine. What a world of difference this would make.

We are naturally drawn to people who bless, even when they are asking for our money! There is a bank near my home that local groups and organizations use for fundraisers. High schools raising funds for their events sometimes use cheerleader squads to attract attention. I noticed that people would give them money because they were passionate about what they were doing. I also noticed that those receiving the most money were not those stating the cause for the fundraiser, but those blessing others by saying, "God bless you." Their message was, "I'm not asking for anything in return or saying what I'm all about, but I'm just blessing you." Attitudes like that separate organizations like The Salvation Army from others. They bless others as they demonstrate the giving heart of God. Most everyone will bless when they are given something as a gesture of thanks. But when we can bless without having received anything in return, then we are getting closer to the heart of the Kingdom of God.

DAD'S PROMISE

As a kid, I remember my dad promising to get my brother, Randy, a horse. He wanted a horse more than I did. I was holding out for a bike.

Taking Randy aside, I warned him, "They are not going to get you a horse. They only want you to take out the trash."

Randy was not easily swayed. "No, they are going to get me a horse!"

"Have you ever had a horse before?" I insisted. "Think man, think!"

But he was still set on getting that horse, so I kept at him. "Just think about it. What makes you think you are ever going to get a horse?"

"You don't know what you are talking about." Randy was defensive.

Soon after my parents got wind of my agitation, Dad assured Randy that in due time, he could have a horse. I had Randy going until the greater authority left no more doubt. By now, I have repented over playing the devil's advocate.

When Randy believed, I no longer had any power or authority over him. Once we choose life and we agree with what God is saying, doubt begins to lose power. By accepting offenses, any word sown into our life through blessings begins to wither away, because offenses seem to take away the hope of anything good happening. We all know that hope deferred makes the heart sick. I had such a conversation with one of my own kids. He was convinced his friend knew what he was talking about and I didn't.

Baffled, I asked, "You're believing your little friend here, who has not lived past 15 years and has never traveled out of the county nor driven a car, over my word?"

His answer was painful. "Well, he knows someone who knew someone who knew someone…."

I knew where this was going. "OK, you go and let him bless you."

Our sustenance flows from whomever we choose to believe. When the Holy Spirit urges us today to not choose the things that oppose the nature of our heavenly Father, it is because He obviously knows better.

The truth about blessing is this—we can either choose to live blessed or cursed. God is not going to force us, and no one is going to twist our arm about it either. Even the Israelites, God's people, had to choose.

> *I call Heaven and earth to witness against you today, that I have set before you **life and death**, the **blessing and the curse**. So choose **life** in order that you may **live**, you and your descendants, by loving the lord your God…this is your life and the length of your days…* (Deuteronomy 30:19-20).

It was one or the other, and they could not have both. To "live" and have "life" means that we are to "come to the fullness of what God intended." God intended an abundant life. A life living in the blessing of God knows no mediocrity. In that position, the blessing of the land is released to us and we enjoy a full life.

God made the blessings so attainable and accessible. Religion makes it seem so impossible and hard to get. But they are reachable and close at hand. Blessings are for here on earth, and God knows we need them.

This commandment which I command you today is not too difficult for you, nor is it out of reach. It is not in Heaven, that you should say, "Who will go up to Heaven for us to get it for us and make us hear it, that we may observe it?" Nor is it beyond the sea, that you should say, "Who will cross the sea for us to get it for us and make us hear it, that we may observe it?" But the word is very near you, in your mouth and in your heart, that you may observe it (Deuteronomy 30:11-14).

When we are born again, we are born into a life of understanding the very nature of God. We short-circuit this when we make it too complicated. The will of God is for us to love Him with our heart, mind, and strength, and out of that comes the structure that we hang the rest of the building on.

And He said to him, "You shall love the Lord your God with all your heart, and with all your soul, and with all your mind" (Matthew 22:37).

From this understanding, we become receptive. The fact of the matter is that we need to know how to receive through blessing. God likes being believed. His words and promises are not up for debate, nor is He going to take them back. God so loved us that He paid the price for our redemption, so we might become all that is a reflection of Him. If we give attention and time to the accuser, then we are delayed on our way to the promise. Our fallen nature bends toward believing the fearful and negative.

When I was a kid, I recall the time I came home from school and told my mom, "So and so said I was ugly."

Overhearing the conversation, my brother piped in, "I've been telling you that for a long time."

Ignoring him, my mom reaffirmed her love for me.

"Look at me!" She said, "I think you are the best thing that ever happened in my life. I was rejoicing the day they told me I had a son." Mother was such a joy. She taught me that I had a choice whether to listen to the kids at school or to the one who loves me. The question is, who are you going to listen to? The answer to that question is the pivot point of success.

Situations that shake us to the core may come. Just like my Starbucks incident. But I learned a life lesson. Mulling over the Starbucks drama was allowing the accuser to become part of my life. By pondering the man's words over and over without any counter words of blessing was debilitating. I was accepting the curse and rejecting the blessing. So I had to do the opposite. God's solution to my dilemma was to meditate on God's promises to me as a son and bless the one who was spewing the curses. Nothing washes and immunizes the mind to the curse like affirmation of a father to a son. So, whether the curses come expectedly or via sneak attack, we can learn to respond in power by blessing. God is good and He is true. If His intentions toward us seem too good to be true, it is because He is good and He is true. Believe what He says about you, and you will prosper and be in health.

PRAYER

Father, bring to mind those things that hold our hearts and minds in chains. Today, we choose life over deadly words, and we choose to believe what You say about us. Since faith comes by hearing, not having heard, we need a hearing word today.

Father, where we have been eating of the tree of the knowledge of good and evil that is cursed, forgive us. Today, we choose to start eating of the tree of life that has an abundance of blessing in its fruit. Thank You that You did not give us what we deserved, but You give us what You desire. Forgive us for rejoicing when ill things happened to others.

BLESSING

Today, I bless the physical well being and break infirmity off of you. The blessing of the Lord is health and fullness. The blessing is not far from you, but it is in your mouth. Be filled with God's favor in all that you bless.

ENDNOTE

1. Biblesoft's New Exhaustive Strong's Numbers and Concordance with Expanded Greek-Hebrew Dictionary. CD-ROM. Biblesoft, Inc. and International Bible Translators, Inc., *biadzo* (971).

CHAPTER EIGHT

THE POWER OF UNITY

It was like a nervous tension that hung over the room. Our scheduled ministry visit to the small Bible school seemed to be ill-timed. There were threats by the neighboring dictator as tensions between the two countries mounted. The saber-rattling consisted of missile testing. Negotiations had broken down, and no one was sure what was going to happen next. The hostility toward Americans only added to the threats. A local Christian newspaper editor asked for an interview. The first question was about the missile threats: "Will America stand with us?" I told him I could not speak for the United States since I was not an ambassador. I could pick up on the anxiety of his persistence for some assurance for his readers. He wanted a confirmation if these threats were a sign of the Last Days.

I told him, "The bigger question is, what will the Christians' response toward the enemy be? Not your enemy toward you."

I was told there was going to be a large gathering of church leaders for the express purpose of praying against the neighboring dictator. I suggested they bless their enemy. He looked at me as if he had misunderstood. Really, he did misunderstand. His grid for blessing was to do something nice for someone, and being nice was the last thing he wanted to do. I explained that Jesus taught in Matthew 5:44 to love your enemies and bless them that curse you. Blessing is not giving them power over you, but instead it is praying over them the will of God. After all, our warfare is not with flesh and blood or by conventional means. I was able to demonstrate what a blessing for a dictator looked like and what God intends for him. He was able to see the difference between what he knew about blessing and the blessing that has power over the enemy.

Later, we were told the prayer gathering changed from praying death on the leader to speaking God's desired intentions over him. I noticed in the news about a week later that the missile threats had stopped and negotiations were opened again. I don't know how much difference the change in praying had made overall, but I do know the difference it makes in the one who adjusts their way of praying to blessing.

THE POWER OF ONE

Ezekiel was by the river when he heard the thunderous noise. He stopped and turned northward to the direction of the commotion. Advancing toward him was a huge storm cloud with a blinding light radiating inside, and then from within emerged four glowing beings. Each creature had four faces and four wings, with lightning dashing madly back and forth among them. Ezekiel knew what this was, and it was no ordinary storm (see Ezek. 1:1-21). This was a heavenly vision. He continued to observe:

> *Whenever they moved, they moved in any of their four directions without turning as they moved. As for their rims they were lofty and awesome, and the rims of all four of them were full of eyes round about. Whenever the living beings moved, the wheels moved with them. And whenever the living beings rose from the earth, the wheels rose also* (Ezekiel 1:17-19).

Amazed, Ezekiel watched as these creatures displayed an extraordinary sense of unity. Each being was powerful and fearful looking but each one followed, *"wherever the spirit was about to go…without turning as they went"* (Ezek. 1:12).

They never broke rank, nor did their heads turn as they moved. Faces pointing outward, they moved with the Spirit of God in that cycling of a wheel within a wheel (see Ezek. 1:15-16). Though in close proximity, none of the beings were tripping over one another, nor was one trying to promote itself over the other. They moved as one. What a perfect picture of unity!

Living and moving in unity as believers invites the Lord to show up. More can be accomplished by unity than not, but it just depends on who is doing the uniting. Unity is an avenue for the release of blessing within a local body. God moves through and within His Body. We are a "cluster" with the potential of being made into new wine (see Isa. 65:8). *Yet break off a grape from the cluster and it becomes a raisin, dried up with no juice.* So, to avoid damaged fruit and to create unity, these ingredients are necessary—proper *connection* to the vine, *consideration* for the ones connected to, *communication* with those who lead you, and *cooperation* for the purpose of the whole harvest.

Get together. Assemble. Meet. That makes *connection* possible (see Heb. 10:25). Learning to get along happens while we fellowship and worship together. Opportunities are fostered there for proper connection to the vine. Part of the participation in corporate fun is learning about one another and allowing others into our lives. Also, we can shift from a mentality of someone owing us to sowing us. We never know when being present in the moment for someone is the difference between life and death.

With connection comes *consideration*—thinking more about how our actions affect those that we connect with. Consideration knows how to function properly in a corporate setting. Consideration is being aware of those around you so they don't feel invisible. How we act in public is different than when we are alone. You can tell if you are considerate or not by how people feel after you have been there. Do you raise the level of peace and joy, or are they exhausted by your company? By understanding proper connection and being considerate of how you fit within the group you will have a sensitivity for how to bless.

Agreement within the local body does not mean that we get everyone on the same page. It is not about everyone doing the same thing, either. Rather, it is about coming into the place we are in agreement with what the Holy Spirit is saying. Walking in agreement simply means we are all looking for the same outcome. People get bogged down with the agreement of methods and lose sight of the final product. Different beliefs and interpretations of the Bible have created enough tensions and dissensions among the cluster which takes away from the ultimate harvest. Worship, for instance, is viewed by some as singing, while others see worship as more experiential. Instead of worship being a dividing point, why not agree with the Scripture, rather than be divided over style?

David gave us a model for worship (see 2 Sam. 6:14-16). He was very demonstrative in his expression of worship to the point of shouts of praise and dancing. If dancing is not part of our background for worship, we tend to disagree with what we have not experienced, even though it is biblical. We can see that agreement is not about what we like as much as it is about getting to the finish line. Being in unity with the Holy Spirit provides for an environment of blessing to overtake you.

Ezekiel's description of the wheel shows how each creature is different with a different perspective, but when they move, those in the back of the wheel must trust the direction, though they are not in the lead. When there is a need for the other creatures to move in the directions they face, then they all move in concert, because the obedience of the group is more important than the individual identity.

Cooperation is working together as a body with the Spirit of the Lord. He leads, we follow. We can be pleasantly surprised at how our personal desires become fulfilled in the process. In a marriage, unity is when a husband and wife are open to the leading of the Holy Spirit and allow Him to move them as one. My wife, Diane, and I don't have to share the same views, but we are still in unity because we are still in union. We both want the same outcome—to please the Lord. Cooperation is simply to act together for the same cause. Without cooperation, there will be no operation of the group. Blessing is a way of bringing together various parts of the Body of Christ to accomplish the harvesting of the fruit. Success or failure for any venture lies in the unity of those who see the end result as more rewarding than any personal agenda.

SCENT OF LIFE

How good and pleasant [how fragrant an odor] *it is for brothers to dwell* [and connect] *together in unity. It is like the precious oil upon the head, coming down upon the beard, even Aaron's beard...* (Psalms 133:1-2).

Unity among brothers is sweet, and yes, this is the way things should be! You could almost hear the longing, or perhaps a sigh, in those words, because when it is there life is pleasant. In its absence, the odor of strife is repulsive even to God. So David, the psalmist and the man after the heart of God, yearned for it. After being anointed as king of a nation, he had the backing of hardcore followers but was on the run from the king he was to replace! Warfare marked his life. Yet David's heart longed for the presence of unity.

He knew that unity created a blend that is agreeable and inviting, wonderful enough to invite God to come among them. Its scent is likened to the smell of the precious anointing oil—God's signature fragrance. Yes, the Lord loves aromas! Moses was instructed to create the scented oil for the purpose of setting apart people and utensils that would be used exclusively for service (see Exod. 30:22-25). The resulting combination of myrrh, cinnamon, cane, cassia, and oil made up a fragrance that was unlike any other. In a robe saturated in this oil, the high priest entered into the Holy of Holies to offer the blood of atonement for covering the people for another year. This anointing oil reminded David of the unity of brethren working together for one purpose. David also said that where unity was, there was also commanded blessing of the Lord. (See Psalm 133:3.)

Notice that unity is an environment that invokes the blessing of God. The anointing oil set a distinction between the common and mundane and the Holy. Those who catch sight of what it means to bless and not curse will most likely experience the unity of the Holy Spirit and an environment that brings favor.

While in London between flights, I ventured into a perfumery. It was not just a store that sold perfume, it was an apothecary of perfumery. I wanted to get some perfume for Diane. I thought it would be very creative on my part to engineer a special blend for her. Picking out the ingredients that I wanted mixed together was quite a challenge. Some of the fragrances that I really liked would not blend with other fragrances that I had chosen. Part way through, the expert perfumer taking the order asked me, "Is this for you?"

"No, it is for my wife."

"Actually," she said, "your wife has to be here so I can match the perfume to her body." She explained to me that everyone's body interacts differently with the fragrances. She said, "I can match it to your body chemistry, but not hers."

This is like the unity of blessing; you have to be present for it to work through you. The commanded blessing can be created in a home by being present with the family so the chemistry of all the different parts can be blended for an aroma that anoints you for special use.

> *And walk in love, just as Christ also loved you and gave Himself up for us, an offering and a sacrifice to God as a **fragrant aroma*** (Ephesians 5:2).

The fragrance is matched to the Body of Christ—believers who will release that aroma. Unity is a sweet aroma, but more than that, it is a powerful combination when mixed with blessing.

David pictured the anointing of unity as the precious oil running down Aaron's beard and settling at the edge of his robe. The place it settled was on the fringes—the most saturated point of the robe. The most potent and powerful aroma of the anointing was not on the head where it is poured, but on the skirt of the garment where it gathers. Just as the river flowing from the throne of God deepened the farther away it flowed from its point of origin, so does the anointing (see Ezek. 47:1-5 NLT). Reaching the saturation point is crucial for the anointing because that is where signs, wonders, and miracles happen.

A certain woman who suffered from the issue of blood found that point of saturation (see Mark 5:25-34). She was sick and she was broke. Her story could be anyone's story. Incurable diseases have the potential to kill hope and clean out savings. But Jesus was in town. Pushing her way into the crowd, she reached out for a miracle and touched the hem of His garment. She found commanded blessing and life flowed into her body, breaking the curse of years of infirmity.

Jesus' early followers also found this saturation point. No doubt the ascension of Jesus into Heaven left a yearning in them for the comfort of His presence. Anticipating the arrival of the Helper that Jesus promised, they waited—120 of them in that upper room (see Acts 2:1-4). Then it happened one day as they were together. The Holy Spirit descended and the anointing of His presence fell upon them. We are now recipients of that saturation of the Lord.

Think of this in terms of releasing blessing. Whenever we bless something or someone, there is a saturation point to be reached for that blessing to take. The challenge is not to give up before we reach it. We do not know, nor do we determine, that point. Consistency is the key. Seemingly stubborn situations or difficult people most likely need more saturation in the blessing, just as we continuously water whatever we want to grow. That targeted blessing saturates the will of God for that person until it is accomplished. God's *rhema* word (the revealed word of God) comes to us as we soak that situation or person with blessing, and He moves the situation from the impossible to the possible. The saturation point is not just for miracles but the place for the flow of blessing. To reach that point, the anointing cannot be hindered.

Where "There" Is

In this particular reference it was called "there." This was the saturation point. It is on the skirts of a garment, the place where the anointing oil naturally concentrated and exactly where God commanded the blessing.

> *It is like the dew of Hermon coming down upon the mountains of Zion; for **there** the Lord commanded the blessing [barak]— life forever* (Psalms 133:3).

So when God said "there," He meant where there is saturation, whether that is of unity or the anointing oil. It is a saturation of blessing.

There is blessing and then there is the commanded blessing. The former is blessing people in a general way. Commanded blessing is specific. It is the Hebrew word, *tsavah* which means "to release or send specifically a message to," someone or something or "to appoint or connect to, or enjoin."[1] So, when I say, "I love you," to my wife, the impact of those words is greater for her than if I say the same to the congregation. Such is the power of an appointed blessing.

"Commanded" also denotes "authority." The commanded blessing carries authority with it so that it will accomplish what it was sent out to do (see Luke 1:37). An angel appearing to Mary announcing that she was going to conceive of the Holy Spirit and give birth to the Messiah pretty much guaranteed that blessing. When the angel said that "nothing" was impossible with God, he was literally saying that, "No fresh spoken word will be without the ability to perform it." A *rhema* word from God has the ability in and of itself to perform what it was assigned to do.

There is an anointing connected with the commanded blessing. It is a powerful anointing to bring life and freedom.

> *The Spirit of the Lord God is upon me, because the Lord has anointed me to bring good news to the afflicted; He has sent me to bind up the brokenhearted, to proclaim liberty to captives and freedom to prisoners* (Isaiah 61:1).

And when Isaiah declared that, *"the spirit of the Lord is upon me,"* he was not saying he was feeling chill bumps. It was more like "to smear with the anointing oil," as was in the case of Aaron when the anointing oil ran down from his head. God's Spirit upon him brought an anointing with specific purposes—to deliver the afflicted, the brokenhearted, the captive, and the prisoner.

Today, believers live under the commanded blessing of the Lord. Our unity becomes the release of that commanded blessing and pleasant aroma before the

Lord. When it comes upon us we begin to smell like Him. It is the scent of blessing with the sweetness of myrrh meaning that we, the believers, have died to ourselves.

We could almost hear the Lord saying, "Aha! The death of My humanity is in this oil. Its sweetness speaks of Me!" It's no wonder that the Lord desires unity among believers.

But just as the Lord is attracted to the aroma of unity, the enemy is invited by the smell of all that is contrary to God. Fear is an odor to the enemy. Anger and unbelief also attract him. If we allow these emotions and feelings to overtake us, the unclean spirits that attach themselves to these encourage us to continually feel that way, if left unchecked. The commanded blessing is not where cursing, division, and strife exist.

THIS WAY UP

What is there in God's treasures for believers to reach maturity and unity? Plenty. God's provision was encompassing and provided full coverage for every stage of that new life. Paul had a revelation of this and wrote about it in the book of Ephesians. This is life in the commanded blessing.

Apostles, prophets, evangelists, pastors, and teachers—commonly termed the fivefold ministry—serve the Body for this particular purpose—to prepare believers for the work of the ministry and to edify them (see Eph. 4:12). Bringing believers to the unity of the faith, maturity, and the knowledge of Jesus is their goal.

> *Till we all come to the unity of the faith and of the knowledge of the Son of God, to a perfect man, to the **measure of the stature of the fullness of Christ**; that we should no longer be **children**, tossed to and fro and carried about with every wind of doctrine, by the trickery of men, in the cunning craftiness of deceitful plotting* (Ephesians 4:13-14 NKJV).

How much of the *"measure of the stature"* we want in all areas of our lives is determined by us—whether we want a lot or little. And the measure is in the *"fullness of Christ."* The word "fullness" is the Greek word *pletho,* which means that "there is no more room to receive, for every nook and cranny is filled."[2] That's full! By setting the measure of blessings that we release from our lives, we also set the measurement for others to bless us in return. The amount of God's power operating within us is determined by the degree that we come into His fullness. This principle works on some level even for the heathen. When they learn to bless others, it keeps on coming back to them.

Maturity is reached when we are no longer acting like children when it comes to our faith. We are no longer tossed around and destabilized in our faith by different opinions. Children are weaker, immature. Their behaviors depend on their moods. One can never tell how they will be each day, whether they will be glad, mad, sad, or whiny. New or immature believers are likened to children. Their foundation is still in the formative stages and therefore unstable. Even the latest doctrine or teaching, no matter how way out there, could excite them. Embracing them like they would a new fad, they can readily accept new things because they lack a deep biblical foundation.

Becoming mature takes time, as does learning to be like Jesus. But God is not in a hurry, because life in His Kingdom is nothing like we have known before.

> But, **speaking the truth** in love, may **grow up** in all things into Him who is the head—Christ—from whom the whole Body, joined and knit together by what every joint supplies, according to the effective working by which every part does its share, causes **growth** of the Body for the edifying of itself in love (Ephesians 4:15-16 NKJV).

God cares about how we communicate with one another. If what He is after is unity, then anything causing schisms or tensions is not pleasing to Him. It is not uncommon for someone to say, "I need to tell you this in love," which is really code for, "I am going to unload on you." Speaking the truth in love was not meant to be the preface for giving someone a piece of our mind. Using this verse as a covering to criticize or straighten someone out is a misuse of Scripture.

Yet speaking the truth in love has nothing to do with filling them in on information. The word "truth" there is the Greek word *alethia*, which means the "manifested reality," or we could say, "Jesus being revealed."[3] Since Jesus is the Way, the Truth, and the Life, it is easy to say Jesus is the Truth. The misconception is for one to think that when they are telling someone the truth, the person listening will grow. The verse read as the one who is speaking truth will grow.

Now, ultimately the one listening to the Truth—Jesus being revealed—will grow as well. Blessing is all about speaking truth as Jesus, the Truth, would have declared it. The one doing the blessing or speaking the truth will grow into the image of Christ. When we are just locked in on the facts of an issue, we may be blinded to the truth. Since truth is what Jesus is saying, facts may be about what the enemy wants us to see, and we end up cursing based on facts. Remember, cursing is placing something or someone in a lower place than Jesus has. Facts tend to do just that—lowering people below the potential that God has set for them. This does not mean we are in denial of the gravity of the situation; it does, however, mean we should not focus solely on what has been, but we should set our attention upon what can be done through blessing.

Cursing is not cussing, but rehearsing the threats to someone what will happen to them if they don't change. Pronouncing failure is a way of cursing or placing them in a lower view than how God sees them. The devil always wants to refer to our past, but God is prophetic—He wants to talk to us about our future. Continual reminders of past failures are a type of cursing because they are the opposite spirit from what Jesus wants to see. Forgiveness was given to us to blot out the past; blessing is prophetic in that it points us to a future destiny and calling.

My friend Bill was told by his father on a regular basis that he was good for nothing and that he would end up in prison. The irony of this cursing was that

Bill did wind up being in jails and prisons. Bill went to law school, became a lawyer, and spent time in prisons interviewing defendants. Bill found Jesus and turned the curse into blessing. One family realized they had been doing a similar thing in rehearsing how bad their son was. They threatened him daily with the consequences of his behavior. His behavior seemed to worsen, just as they had been predicting. After getting understanding of blessing, they realized they had been cursing their son and lowering him to a place of despair. Just days after mending their ways to blessing they saw a difference in his attitude toward others. Now their son is learning to be a blesser.

We were designed to be people that grow in response to love. Providing the right environment for something to grow is critical. *Grow* is the potential to come into what something was originally designed to become. A combination of the right ingredients enables a plant to grow because of its DNA. Provide all the right conditions and the environment will happily release the potential of the seed. Seed bears in itself the blueprint for its future. Right conditions for a believer to grow include speaking the truth in love and the watering of the Word.

> *Since you have in obedience to the truth purified your souls for a sincere love of the brethren, fervently love one another from the heart, for you have been born again not of seed which is perishable but imperishable, that is, through the living and enduring Word of God* (1 Peter 1:22-23).

Being born again means that we have new seed or DNA. God set the principle of how the seed works in the Genesis account of creation. God said the life is in the seed. We have been given life inside the seed of Christ that abides in us. Blessing waters the seed so it comes to its potential of full life. Cursing destroys faith and discourages the soul in becoming God's building.

Since we are responsible to provide an environment for growth through blessing or cursing, any conditions hindering or stifling that growth—such as demonic powers that thrive on cursing—need to be removed. They can cause the condition or environment to stagnate or fail to produce growth. Whether that is within a church, family, or work atmosphere, dealing with unfavorable conditions to a person's growth is paramount. Caring for the health and growth of today's church means that we learn to bless and not just give information. That is, we bless with the truth, for blessing with the truth encourages spiritual maturity. Ultimately, we grow to a place where we are like Jesus, who exhibited a deep, unwavering trust in His Father.

I was asked to pray for a lady who had been having severe health issues. I started to pray, and she kept interrupting the prayer with more information. Mostly it was what the doctors were saying. I began again, and before I could get to the declaration of healing she wanted to tell me that the doctors said she could die from this. This lady was so focused on the information given to her she could not hear the pronouncing of the blessing of healing. The seeds of death were so planted in such a way she could not help but water them every chance she got. I was able to ask her to listen to the word and set her heart on living and not dying. She is still with us today. I have no problem with doctors telling a patient the facts, but when we believe God for a miracle we must set aside the information and hear the blessing of transformation.

> *For this reason I bow my knees to the Father of our Lord Jesus Christ, from whom the whole family in Heaven and earth is named, that He would **grant** you, according to the riches of His glory, **to be strengthened with might through His Spirit in the inner man,** that Christ may dwell in your hearts through faith*... (Ephesians 3:14-17 NKJV).

The word *grant* means, "Here is my God-given potential, or what my intention is." Again, God has good intentions toward each one of us. Seeing that God-given potential come into fruition for someone is a cause for celebration. Paul also understood that strength in our inner person is vital. We are strengthened in the inner person through blessing. Blessing is good medicine for the soul. Blessing is God's power coming through the Holy Spirit in the inner person.

> *...That you, being rooted and grounded in love, may be able to comprehend with all the saints what is the **width and length***

and depth and height —*to know the love of Christ which passes knowledge; that you may be filled with all the **fullness of God*** (Ephesians 3:17-19 NKJV).

The *"fullness of God"* encompasses all four dimensions—width, length, depth, and height. Length and breadth alone are not fullness. We need all four aspects. By becoming like Christ in every aspect of our lives, we begin to live life like He did—as overcomers of the world. Consequently, we no longer specialize in one aspect of our faith, such us only ministering faith or healing. We can function in every aspect of Christ. That is because, as the Body of Christ, we respond to the will of the Head—Christ.

We become blessers, just like Jesus. We begin to look at people and life through His eyes of grace and hear things the way He hears. That is the unity of the spirit in the *"bond of peace"* (see Eph. 4:3). A concerted movement together of Christ's body can bring an unparallel release of the glory of God. Such an environment invites God to show up and do the impossible. It enables us to repel demonic powers, heal the sick, cast out demons, and invoke the blessing of God.

PRAYER

Lord, we are so thankful that You have given us a freshly spoken word to bless the Body and the house of the Lord. God, we want to get this inside of us. If we don't get anything else, we want to get this down into our spirit. Let it not be just another message that comes and goes and tickles our ears, but let it become part of the fiber of who we are as those who bless what You bless. We want to be connected to Your cluster and be a blessing to those we are connected to.

ENDNOTES

1. Biblesoft's New Exhaustive Strong's Numbers and Concordance with Expanded Greek-Hebrew Dictionary. CD-ROM. Biblesoft, Inc. and International Bible Translators, Inc., *tsavah* (6680).

2. Strong's, *pletho* (4130).

3. Strong's, *alethia* (225).

PART IV

Manifestation of

BLESSING

CHAPTER NINE

NO MORE GOPHERS

Genesis records the account of creation. After each segment of creation, God blessed it and said it was good (see Gen. 1:25). The creation of man was the only time in creation that God not did not declare it was good. In fact, He said it was not good for man to be alone.

The test of blessing came when my brother Joe, living in Amarillo, Texas, was having trouble with gophers ruining his lawn. The critters would tunnel underground, eating the fresh roots of the grass. He did the normal things one does to rid gophers. He tried poisoning them, only to find them getting fatter. The tunnels seem to get wider while he was getting more frustrated with them. He bought special traps for the little diggers. They seem to dig around the traps and continued destroying his yard. He even tried cursing the rodents, thinking he had authority over them. He was told I was teaching on blessing what God created.

His first thought was, "You can't bless an animal, much less one that is being destructive." Since the other methods were not working, he decided to give it a try. One evening while no one was watching, he went outside and said something to the effect of, "Mr. Gopher, I don't know why God made you, but I know it wasn't to destroy my lawn, so I bless you to fulfill the purpose for which you were created and I release you to go to greener pastures." He tromped down all the tunnels to see if it would truly work. To his amazement, the next day there were no more signs of tunneling. He blessed them right out of his yard.

Some might think, "Come on now, a gopher? Really?" When we bless what God has blessed then we are in agreement with Him. I was sharing the gopher story in Serbia, and the pastor who was translating for me thought that I had said "girlfriend" instead of "gopher," and without missing a beat, he translated: "The pastor's girlfriend tore up the backyard!" Thankfully, his wife, who knew more English, caught the blooper and translated it correctly. After a good laugh, they caught the principle of blessing even when it seems foolish to do so.

I shared the same story with a group of prisoners in a federal penitentiary in southern Texas. I told them they could bless the guards instead of cursing them. A few weeks later, I got a report through the chaplain's office of an amazing story. One of the cell blocks had been overrun with roaches. They seemed to not be able to exterminate them for very long at a time. They decided to do what my brother did with the gophers. They got together and blessed the roaches as God's creation, not knowing why they were created, but simply because they belonged to the Lord. In a short time, the roaches had moved out of their cell block to another one. These men learned firsthand the power that is in blessing. I have at least two other reports of people hearing these testimonies and trying it out on their gophers, only to find that it really works.

GOODBYE, BEAVERS!

If it works with gophers, it must work with beavers, Holly reasoned. She was listening to me talk about blessing gophers and remembered she was having trouble with beavers. Eight long months of trying to clear her property of beavers was getting to her. She had already tried shooting the beavers without success. She had tried calling the wildlife conservation people, who told her she was number 55 on the list and it would be several months before they could trap the beavers. She recalled how the beavers had already become a costly nuisance. They had taken down a huge number of trees on the property; they had built themselves a nice dam across her pond! Their burrowing had caused a leak in the dam that threatened to flood a county road and other nearby properties. But she was not going to let that happen. Not after hearing about blessing what God had created. Leaving service that Sunday, she decided God was not a respecter of persons or animals, and it would not hurt to try blessing the pests. Nothing else had worked.

Quickly surveying her surroundings, she was assured that there was no one else around in her land. She was alone with the beavers. *Here goes…*

"I just bless you beavers to the next pond."

Her voice echoed in the quietness, bringing home a realization. Should the beavers move to one of her neighbor's ponds, they could experience agonizing months like she did. That was something she did not wish on anyone.

She recanted, "Oh, I don't want you to ruin someone else's pond. I just bless you to the heavenlies, and I bless you out of here to a better life!"

By now, she was yelling at the top of her voice, mostly out of frustration. The next day, the beavers were still there. She must have thought, "Well, it worked for others but not for me." A few days had passed when she got a call from the head of the Extension Service in Fort Worth, Texas, the department that deals with animal control. Yes, the head of the Extension Service! He was informing her that her name was next on the list to come and remove the beavers. He could not explain how she got moved up on the list, but she was next. After eight months of contacting the proper county authorities and even the Extension Service with no success, this was a mountain-moving experience!

RULING THE CONQUERED

Conquests are exciting for the conquerors. But ruling may be another story. The greater challenge between the two is to rule, because that calls for the continual dominance of whatever was conquered. Ever heard of a man who can make a million dollars but cannot keep it? Money rules the man. Though he can conquer the idea of making money, he cannot rule money. What we can conquer but cannot rule produces frustration and disappointment. Cycles of constant ups and downs in a Christian's life may be a reflection of that reality. This is true in our external and internal worlds.

> *He who is slow to anger is better than the mighty, and he who rules*
> *his spirit, than he who captures a city* (Proverbs 16:32-32).

Solomon wrote Proverbs, and he understood something about ruling. Ruling ourselves is first priority. Whatever we need to overcome, remember there is a reign to follow which determines longevity. If we cannot rule ourselves, we are sure to lose any ground we gained. The length of our stay in the place we conquered is determined by whether we can rule.

> *Like a city that is broken into and without walls is a man who*
> *has no control over his spirit* (Proverbs 25:28).

The picture is of a city without protection. When we think of this in regards to our life, any inability to govern ourselves becomes an invitation for the enemy to harass and exact a toll on us, drawing us to the curser's side. This is a matter of having self-control and keeping our emotions in check, especially anger. We are responsible for how we respond to life's surprises. The enemy of our soul will be more than happy to control our emotions if we let him. He has sought to rule over our emotions since the Garden of Eden. In that place of perfection and innocence, the serpent was able to find an inroad into the heart of man through sin. Jesus Christ, through His death and resurrection, restored the power to conquer and rule, beginning with ourselves. But the struggle is still ongoing.

Even before humankind, satan wanted to rule everything. He was not just set on conquering; he was vying for the right to rule. Rebelling against God with a third of the angels was the result of his pride. His rebellion against God, however, cost him his place in Heaven, and he was cast down to earth. It was one of several times that the devil would be thrown out of Heaven.

> *By the abundance of your trade you were internally filled with violence, and you sinned; therefore I have cast you as profane from the mountain of God. And I have destroyed you, O covering cherub, from the midst of the stones of fire. Your heart was lifted up because of your beauty; you corrupted your wisdom by reason of your splendor. I cast you to the ground; I put you before kings, that they may see you* (Ezekiel 28:16,17).

Isaiah penned another time when lucifer, the son of the dawn, was expelled to earth.

> *How you have fallen from Heaven, O star of the morning, son of the dawn! You have been cut down to the earth, you who have weakened the nations!* (Isaiah 14:12)

The book of Revelation gives us a peek into the conflict in Heaven. It was a heavenly place where satan could enter and make accusations to the Lord against believers. Scripture refers to lucifer or satan as *"the prince of the power of the air"* (Eph. 2:2).

> *And there was war in Heaven, Michael and his angels waging war with the dragon. The dragon and his angels waged war, and they were not strong enough, and there was no longer a **place** found for them in Heaven. And the great dragon was thrown down, the serpent of old who is called the devil and Satan, who deceives the whole world; he was thrown down to the earth, and his angels were thrown down with him* (Revelation 12:7-9).

Satan lost the war in Heaven and was cast down to Earth, which before the creation was called the planet of darkness. That heavenly place that he had access to was no longer available to him. The word place in Revelation 12 means "land." It is the same word "place" in Ephesians where Paul told believers not to *"give place to the devil"* (see Eph. 4:27 NKJV). The word "land" here is the word *topos*, where we get the word "topography."[1] In essence, the devil lost any ground to stand on in Heaven. God loves land. It is no wonder that He is so jealous over the land of Israel. He encourages His people to buy the land, keep the land, and hold the land. The parable of the "Pearl of Great Price" tells of the need to buy the land that the pearl was buried in. It is one thing to overcome, but then it is up to us not to give any more ground—not a handhold, toehold, or foothold—to the devil. Glance back to the Israelites' entrance to the Promised Land. In order to rule that land, they had to drive out the Canannites, the Perizzites, and any other pagan idol worshipers (see Josh. 3:10). Coexisting with them was not an option. Blessing and cursing cannot live side by side.

James writes that blessing and cursing should not come out of the same mouth any more than sweet and bitter water can come from the same fountain (see James 3:10-11).

> *Now the salvation, and the power, and the Kingdom of our God and the authority of His Christ have come, for the **accuser of our brethren** has been thrown down, he who accuses them before our God day and night* (Revelation 12:10).

The devil may have lost his place in Heaven, but he looks for places in earthen vessels from which he can curse God and His family. He does not cease to accuse us to the Father. "Accuser" is a way of saying "curser." Satan is the curser of God's children. When one is pronouncing failure and judgment upon another it is in the category of being an accuser. It is no wonder that God is not pleased with us when we curse someone. Satan lost his place in Heaven as an accuser. We can certainly miss out on the favor of God through cursing what God has blessed.

The devil's list of accusations and questionings are endless: "How could You love them? Don't You see what they did? How could You deliver and save a people that turn their back on You? How could You treat someone so mercifully when they are so cold toward You?" Satan is a legalist—he looks for cracks to accuse us as unfaithful or disobedient. He will work through others to pronounce judgments of condemnation on us. Psalms says blessed is the one that does not sit in the seat of the scoffer (see Ps. 1:1). Blessed are those who choose another seat than the seat of the scoffer. *Scoffing* means to belittle or make small something that has value. Cursing is similar in that it devalues what God has blessed. If you find yourself without blessing, maybe you should evaluate your seating arrangements.

THE BLOOD THAT SPEAKS

Since the devil roams around the earth looking for those who are easy prey, we have to deal with his schemes. But we are not without protection from his derogatory slams, nor do we lack power to defeat him.

> *And they overcame him because of the **blood of the Lamb** and because of the **word of their testimony,** and they did not love their life even when faced with death* (Revelation 12:11).

The blood of Jesus is the protection and the word of our testimony is a weapon. In the above Scripture, "word" can be translated as either *rhema* or *logos.* "Testimony" is the word *marturia,* which means to "give evidence to something of a greater reality."[2] The believers gave evidence that they were saying the same thing as God. Their testimony is the same as when Jesus was on the earth. Jesus, when confronting the devil in the mountain, used the Word; He testified by saying, "It is written." The blood of Jesus was the payment in full that has set a barrier between the family of God and the devil. When we say what Jesus has said in His Word and claim our inheritance because of His blood, we have the power to defeat the devil. The devil cannot take any ground where we are blessing—saying what Jesus would say. The battle is won through the blood of the Lamb and blessing what Jesus has blessed through His sacrifice. He is the ultimate Victor and rightful Ruler of all that He conquered. Jesus overcame sin, the world, death, and the accuser.

This principle of having a claim backed up by something greater is reflected in our monetary system. Paper money has no value in itself. The dollar is a claim that something greater backs it. The United States has not been on the gold standard for many years, yet the strength of the country backs the value of the dollar.

I learned this principle firsthand at an early age, dealing with bullies in sixth grade. Perhaps it was because I was not very tall (I did not bloom until I was 17) or maybe it was my mouth. I didn't feel confident in my skills as a fighter, but I did feel confident in my older brother, Randy. Randy would turn into a buzz saw if provoked with the right words. I told my nemeses that if they touched me I would tell my brother. They would reply, "We don't know your brother, and we are not afraid of him."

Well, that was because they had never seen Randy. Randy was a pretty good-sized guy. His size alone usually was enough to convince any of my enemies. One day after school, one of the bullies cornered me. I usually was able to avoid them, but not today. I was doing my best to hold him off with running my mouth, which was the only defense I had at the moment. Randy was due at any time to come around the corner to pick me up. It seemed he was running a little late today. Of all the times for him to be late!

Finally, he came. I was to the point where I was backed up against the door of the school building. I was trying to remember those movies where Billy Jack whips a whole motorcycle gang. The bully was close enough that I could feel his hot breath. Then, just like the cavalry in those Western movies, I heard Randy's car. His 1963 Impala had dual Hollywood mufflers that were distinct. I hollered, "Randy, he wants to whip you!"

Randy assessed the situation in mere seconds and jumped out of the car. That bully took one look at this bull charging him and took off running without looking back. I felt really stout at that point, but it dawned on me that my name did not mean anything until my brother showed up. I never had any more problems with that bully the rest of that year.

Eventually, I graduated and went on to junior high school, where no one knew my brother.

Sometime afterward I hinted to Randy, "You have to come by my school and meet some of my friends."

"You are on your own this year," remarked Randy. "You are going to have to fight your own battles." I soon realized it wasn't enough for me to conquer, I had to rule. First, I had to conquer my mouth before I could rule anything. I am only as strong as the blood of Jesus and my testimony of blessing.

Imagine the powers of darkness on the morning of Jesus' resurrection. When they saw Jesus rising out of the grave, they knew what Big Brother looked like! They understood the authority and power of the blood of Jesus. The Bible names Jesus as the First Born among many brothers. Jesus is my big brother in the family of God (see Rom. 8:29). That blood continues to speak today. Every demon knows that the blood covering is over every believer in Christ, and it validates their claim to overcome and rule as believers. When a believer declares the power of the blood, its authority is released.

Jesus possessed the authority to not just whip the devil but the authority to rule over him for eternity. Satan attempted to get Jesus to use His authority to satisfy His own hunger. After fasting 40 days, Jesus was hungry. Satan offered all the kingdoms of the earth for one moment of worship or the temptation to turn the stones into bread. Jesus answered quoting from the book of Deuteronomy, *"It is written, man shall not live on bread alone, but on every word that proceeds out of the mouth of God"* (Matt. 4:4).

Though Jesus had the authority and power to turn the stones into bread, He chose not to use His authority for the flesh.

Overcoming has nothing to do with how cleverly we phrase our words or how loud we can holler at the devil. God's inspired and inerrant Word that has passed thousands of years of testing is our weapon of choice.

Hanging between Heaven and earth on that Cross, Jesus was faced with the choice of cursing or blessing. I think satan thought he had Jesus defeated. With the crowd wanting the execution of an innocent man, along with the taunts of *"He saved others but He can't save Himself,"* Jesus chose to bless them even from the Cross. With His last breath He asked for forgiveness on their behalf. We really know the power of blessing is a reality when we can bless while being confronted with shouts of cursing. Jesus overcame with His blood and the word of blessing.

It was as if satan was taunting Him and saying, "Come on, curse me. Do You see what they have done to You? You came to Your own people and they did not receive You. Look at You; You are nailed."

Jesus saw the eternal plan and *"for the joy set before Him endured the Cross"* (Heb. 12:2). Jesus looked past the moment of cursing and pain and saw the glory that He had in the beginning with the Father. If we could at times look past the circumstantial evidence against us and see what happens when we bless, I think we'd be able to endure a little longer before taking the bait to curse. Pleasing the Father was better than getting out of the momentary pain. Though Heaven awaited His command to come to His rescue (that option was certainly available to Him), Jesus refused to use His authority for self-gratification. We are today victorious because He blessed and did not curse that day on the Cross. Our authority through the blood of Jesus is uncontested.

WINNING THROUGH BLESSING

Many messages perpetuate the lie that cursing people and things may produce results, but they are not the results that honor God. Yet people are buying into this in their desperate search for change and power.

A book was circulating around Serbia that promoted the idea of cursing whomever or whatever you did not like. Written by an American man, the book had been translated into Serbian and Hungarian. Church people were cursing anyone they disliked, including cars and trees! Fear was the driving force behind this motivation. Cursing looks for destruction for its determined fruit. Blessing looks for restoration and resolution as the measure of its success.

Are you a *determinator* (my play on words)—a *terminator* when it comes to blessing? A determinator is determined to bless no matter what anyone does in return. They are not moved by the immediate circumstances. A terminator has linear thinking and cuts off a relationship when there is any hint of resistance. The determinator will win out through blessing. A terminator has a lot of burned bridges and numerous short-term relationships. If it is worth fighting for, it is worth blessing to win. At the very least, blessing is close to the heart of the Lord, and you will feel the pleasure of the Lord when you bless and refrain from cursing. With the small snapshot of Stephen we are given in the book of Acts, we get the picture that he had the heart of a determinator.

He was a deacon that served in benevolence. Stephen was full of faith and of the Holy Spirit (see Acts 6:5). Stephen's ministry was powerful enough to get the attention of the religious people due to the signs and miracles that were happening through his ministry. He confounded the religious leaders with the spirit of wisdom and the spirit in which he was speaking. They were so threatened by losing control of their domain that they set a conspiracy against Stephen. Dreaming up false accusations, they had Stephen dragged before the religious council to stand trial there. In his defense, Stephen recounted the history of the Jews and ended with a scalding rebuke of the religious hearers.

> *You men who are stiff-necked and uncircumcised* [outside of covenant] *in heart and ears are always resisting* [set on what you believe and will not hear] *the Holy Spirit; you are doing just as your fathers did* [living under a generational curse]. *Which one of the prophets did your fathers not persecute? They killed those who had previously announced the coming of the Righteous One, whose betrayers and murderers you have now become; you who received the law as ordained by angels, and yet did not keep it* (Acts 7: 51-53).

After that public address, Stephen's audience was fit to be tied. Spurred by their hatred of the truth and the man who dared to say it, they rushed at him gnashing their teeth—not a pleasant sight. In their mind, there was one way to silence such a man and that was death. But Stephen gazed up to Heaven and saw the glory of God. Jesus was standing at the right hand of the Father.

> *"Behold, I see the heavens opened up and the Son of Man standing at the right hand of God." But they cried out with a loud voice, and covered their ears and rushed at him with one impulse. When they had driven him out of the city, they began*

stoning him; and the witnesses laid aside their robes at the feet of
a young man named Saul (Acts 7:56-58).

This is a mature believer filled with faith and determination. Surrounded by his adversaries and on the verge of death, he did not react to the crowd's hatred. Instead of gnashing back at the people and cursing them for their rejection, Stephen saw Jesus and blessed them by pronouncing the will of God, which was to forgive them. In my mind I picture Stephen catching sight of Jesus, the epitome of blessing, and then doing what he saw Jesus doing. Wow! That will get the endorphins flowing.

> *Then falling on his knees, he cried out with a loud voice, "Lord,*
> *do not hold this sin against them!" Having said this, he fell asleep*
> (Acts 7:60).

What a powerful thing! Stephen fought against the natural human tendency to withhold blessing and forgiveness from the mob. He didn't call out and say, "Lord Jesus, get me out of this mess! I did not bargain for this," or, "I've been just serving food; don't I deserve some perk out of this?" Stephen saw the One who broke the power of the curse, so his focus was not set on the accusers but the blesser. Instead, his glimpse of the Lord in His glory gave him strength to bless the conspirators and executioners. Stephen became a witness to the truth that greater is He who blesses than he who curses.

We never know who we affect when we choose a blessing stance. Paul the apostle, a man whom God greatly used to write a third of the New Testament, was at the stoning of Stephen as a young man. That event had to have made an impression on Paul's (Saul at the time) mind (see Acts 22:20). Later on, when Paul was faced with angry, resistant people, he also chose to bless and not curse.

On another occasion, Paul and Silas were beaten and thrown into prison for giving a young slave girl freedom from a spirit of divination. Paul and Silas began singing praise to the Lord instead of complaining about their accommodations. Other prisoners listened to them pray and sing hymns. Then suddenly, at about midnight, the jail experienced an earthquake that caused the prison doors to open. Revival broke out and the jailer and his entire household were saved. While other prisoners were cursing their captors, Paul and Silas became the thermostat for the rest of the jail and changed the temperature from cold-hearted to a red-hot revival. You can change your situation if you will bless at all times and let His praise be continually in your mouth.

When we are waiting on the Holy Spirit there is much that we go through. The time frame varies. An important development took place for me recently.

Twenty-two years ago, I was betrayed in a court of law and my family was at stake. Although I had long since forgiven and released the people who plotted against my family, my wife and I recently felt that we needed to bless them. We began to declare, "Lord let them come into favor with You. Let them experience the reality of Your grace."

Now, twenty-plus years later, they call, asking me for some help. They brought up the issue and asked for forgiveness for what they had done in court that day. Was I blessing them twenty-plus ago? No. I was saying, "God let there be justice," or at least what I deemed as justice. I think resolution would have come years earlier had I practiced blessing.

Blessing is a final step in forgiveness. I can forgive every day, but when I bless I can begin to see them through the eyes of their Creator and Father. Somehow, things begin to look differently. When you bless people you can feel their heart. It is as if the Lord pulls back the reality covers and we can see things from another vantage point. From the vantage point of the heavenly Father it is amazing how you can see in light of eternity. As the years passed, I felt passive about the betrayal issue I had faced. Yet the more I blessed them, the more I felt mercy for them. That is truly the power of blessing.

We are not alone in our struggle in this world. Nor are we without hope. Winning through blessing was the way Jesus overcame.

> *In this world you will have tribulation; but be of good cheer, I [Jesus] have overcome the world* (John 16:33 NKJV).

When we find that we are constantly blaming other people for issues, whether it is on the job or at home, there is a good chance we have not grasped the revelation of blessing. Blessing means that in the midst of chaos we can still see Jesus and we bless. Hearing about someone else's pain and suffering or what they are saying about us is only bait the enemy uses for cursing. Carrying the spirit of cursing is like being a magnet—you attract more of the same. Also, your vision is skewed from seeing the goodness of the Lord. Cursing pushes the pause button and we are frozen in time, held back from moving into our destiny or divine favor.

MAKING THE U-TURNS

"Nothing ever connected," the lady said through her tears. But she continued to testify and repent before the church. Life had been a bitter pill. I had seen the hollow look in her eyes many times before—the look of one who has lost hope of the miracle happening.

She had experienced her share of disappointments. At this juncture in life, she had moved from hopeful to survivor mode. That was how she was taught by her parents to think and look at life. Her life was marked by anger directed at God and other people, and don't even bring up the church, because as far as she was concerned she was just attending because the rest of the family was there.

Then, that night in the meeting, she heard the message of the power of blessing. Her countenance was noticeably different. She asked if she could share something. Getting the OK from the pastor, I agreed. She began by asking the church to forgive her for the distant attitude she had shown to everyone. She repented to the pastor for resistance to his leadership and the occasional gossip of discontent. She readily admitted that, until that night, "I did not know I had been cursing the church and most of the people in it."

It was evident that this was her freedom moment. The realization that things could change for her fueled hope for the first time in many years. Her admission was so dramatic to those who knew her that it started to catch on when another lady followed suit. She had been cursing her family, especially her husband. She blamed him for all the problems they were facing. She questioned if God could ever do anything good in his life. Not until that night could she expect any change. She, too, quickly repented to her husband and to the whole church for her actions and for being in agreement with a cursing spirit.

That night, the place was full, and one could sense the expectation building. God's presence descended upon the place like a tent covering us when repentance broke out. People were on their faces repenting to God and to one another.

I was directed to give a word prophetically to a young man at the back. The word was that there was unfinished business in his life that he needed to take care of before he would be able to do what was really in his heart. I relayed the message. Later on, I found out that he had been instrumental in dividing the church years earlier and had taken seventy people with him. (He was on staff at the time.) He went straight to the pastor and repented for what he had done. Sometimes when the revelation of blessing is introduced, it is preceded with repentance to break the repetitive cycles of cursing.

PRAYER

Father, I thank You for the power of the Holy Spirit that allows us to enter into the blessing of the Lord. At this very moment, we want to be free from those words that have hurt and wounded us. We know that nothing can bring division and strife unless we give it life. We ask that the power of Your grace would deliver us and cause us to be an instrument of blessing in word and in deed. Amen.

ENDNOTES

1. Biblesoft's New Exhaustive Strong's Numbers and Concordance with Expanded Greek-Hebrew Dictionary. CD-ROM. Biblesoft, Inc. and International Bible Translators, Inc., *topos* (5117).

2. Strong's, *marturia* (3141).

CHAPTER TEN

———❖———

YOUR REDEMPTION DRAWS NEAR

In the previous chapters, we have discussed the benefits of blessing—it honors the Lord as well as releases our inheritance in the Lord. I must confess, like most people, I used to use the term *blessing* to describe a feeling or a state of being. If someone was doing well and things were going their way, they would say, "I am blessed." I have since come to realize blessing is a lifestyle and a position of being covered by the favor of the Lord. However, we must distinguish the feeling of blessing from the obedience of blessing. We can do this by comparing the words "happy" and "joy."

Happiness is based solely upon happenings. It is an emotion or feeling we get when what is happening in our life is agreeable. When something good like a promotion comes, we are happy. Joy, on the other hand, is an attribute of the Holy Spirit. It is not based on the need for something happy to rejoice about. The Bible says the joy of the Lord is our strength (see Neh. 8:10). Notice that it does not say the joy *for* the Lord. The joy comes as a direct impartation from the Lord through the Holy Spirit. This kind of joy is a result of trusting the Lord in every happening of life. The joy of the Lord is a constant, even while things are not necessarily happy. Happiness may be momentary or fleeting at best, but the joy of the Lord is the sense that God is control, even though I don't understand it at the moment.

Blessing is similar because it is not based on thing like whether we feel like we are blessed or in fact don't feel like blessing anyone. Blessing should be a constant in our life much like joy is. Blessing is also an attribute of Christ; after all, He died to free those who were under a curse. Blessing is not about a feeling—whether someone we don't particularly like deserves to be blessed or not. I am thankful that Jesus did not wait to get the right feeling before He was willing to die for me.

I don't think Jesus was necessarily happy about going to the Cross. We can see this by the prayer He prayed in the Garden—for the cup He had to drink to pass from Him if possible. Jesus also prayed, *"…Not My will* [happiness], *but Yours be done"* (Luke 22:42). We also read in Hebrews 12:2 that Jesus—the Author and Finisher of our faith—endured the Cross for the joy set before Him. We can see that the joy He saw kept Him moving toward His destiny. I believe the joy Jesus saw was the glory that was going to be restored to Him at the right hand of the Father after the Cross.

Sometimes blessing may feel like having to die to our own will. However, the joy that follows is the power of God released to do His will—to bless and not curse. Resurrection is connected to blessing. The resurrection is the victory that gives every believer the authority to resist the devil. Blessing is the victory whereby we did not fall prey to cursing or passing judgment on who deserves our blessing. Blessing is like forgiveness—it is a gift that we can give. That is why we can forgive as a gift, or we can hold it and not be forgiven ourselves. Like blessing, we can give it as a gift or we can withhold blessing and choose not to receive it either. Jesus gave us the gift of life through the resurrection, and we, through the power of blessing, can choose life over death, blessing over cursing. The power of blessing is truly of the redemptive kind.

Nothing Takes the Place of Obedience

Jonah the prophet received an assignment from God to go to the city of Nineveh. There, he was to preach repentance and leave the rest up to God.

Jonah did not feel like going to Nineveh, knowing that they would repent and God would turn from His wrath. Jonah evidently preferred to see the fireworks as opposed to the mercy of God. Like some of us, Jonah wanted a confirmation to his feelings. He went down to the pier and coincidently found a ship going in the opposite direction of Nineveh—the direction that he was fleeing.

Jonah was happy now because he had things going his way; though he felt like cursing Nineveh, he had peace about the whole situation. I know this because Jonah was able to go down into the boat and fall fast asleep. I should note that there is a peace that we can conjure up to agree with our own disobedience. One can be at peace in their mind but not be at peace in their spirit. It wasn't until Jonah found himself swallowed by a giant fish and then thrown up on a beach that he realized blessing is redemptive and cursing is rebellion.

Speaking of redemption, the Holy Spirit reminded me of the last time Jesus ate Passover with His disciples. It was emphasized with His putting forth the cup of redemption. Let me first give some brief history about this powerful moment with His disciples. Jesus' declaration that night at the Passover meal (the Jewish feast) took on new meaning. There is so much more to this covenant meal than what the average communion service encompasses. For this writing, a small explanation relevant to blessing will have to suffice.

CUP OF BLESSING

There were four cups of wine at one feast. This was the Jewish Passover. During this feast, four cups of wine were drunk to commemorate the Israelites' journey as a people and God's promise to them. The first cup of wine was taken to remember what the Lord had done. Coming out of Egypt to the Promised Land was an event never to be forgotten. No other people saw the protection and provision of God as strongly as the Israelites.

Pouring a small amount of wine into the cup, the Jews drank it and stated something to this effect: "Lord, we remember that You brought us out of Egypt."

The second cup of wine was drunk as a remembrance that they would never be slaves again. Years of backbreaking labor in Egypt were to be a memory and only that. Then the third cup, the one most people are familiar with because of communion, was the one with which Jesus chose to make His prophetic declaration. This was the *cup of redemption*, also known as the *cup of blessing—eulogia* in Greek—and the *cup of the Trinity*.[1] I'll explain more in a moment.

The fourth cup of wine symbolized the prophetic promise given to Abraham that they would be a people and a nation. God has not forgotten His promise to Israel. The more anti-Semitic the world becomes, the more Israel will know that Jehovah is God.

The Israelites' story of deliverance from Egypt was ratified in that third cup. It was viewed as the blood of the lamb! Smeared over the doors of the Israelites' homes, the blood kept them safe from the spirit of death that moved through Egypt, taking the firstborn who were not covered by the blood (see Exod. 12:13). The Egyptians came under judgment by being cursers that defrauded and enslaved the Israelites. God had promised Abraham that He would bless those who blessed him and curse those who cursed him (see Gen. 12:3). This certainly held true for Abraham's seed as well. The Egyptians were experiencing the God of Abraham returning their curses back on them. The telling and retelling of the deliverance story was now the Israelites' mandate for generations to come. Their enemies heard of their miraculous freedom. It struck fear in their hearts. Who wanted to go to war with a nation whose God cared for them like that?

How prophetic it was for Jesus to choose the third cup at the Passover meal! With the cup of redemption, He announced a new covenant between God and humanity. Jesus could have chosen any of the four cups for remembrance, but He chose the cup of redemption. Paul refers to this cup as the *Cup of Blessing* (see 1 Cor. 10:16). The cup Jesus drank from—or, in a truer sense, the cup He would demonstrate—was the crucifixion.

I think it is interesting that this "Cup of the Cross," if you will, was called the Cup of Blessing. Jesus went to the Cross of Blessing to set us free from the power of cursing. This principle of blessing is still relevant today; within it, we can break the power of a curse through the power of a blessing. Blessing always triumphs over cursing.

Which side of the Cross are you on? The side of blessing that destroys the curse, or the side of the curse that is in opposition to the work of the Cross? This covenant represented the heart of the Father—a heart of blessing. It was a better covenant. Jesus also made the connection between the cup of blessing and the blood of the lamb. The connection is that when we take the cup of blessing we come under the new covenant. Gone is the veil that separated us from God; we can now have access to all of God's promises. What they had in the Old Testament was a mere shadow of it.

> *Speak to all the congregation of Israel, saying, "On the tenth of this month they are each one to take a lamb for themselves, according to their fathers' households, **a lamb for each household.** Now if the household is too small for a lamb, then he and his neighbor nearest to his house are to take one according to the number of persons in them; according to what each man should eat, you are to divide the lamb. Your lamb shall be an unblemished male a year old; you may take it from the sheep or from the goats. You shall keep it until the fourteenth day of the same month, then the whole assembly of the congregation of Israel is to kill it at twilight. Moreover, **they shall take some of the blood and put it on the two doorposts and on the lintel of the houses in which they eat it"** (Exodus 12:3-7).*

The Israelites had to choose a lamb without defect for the Passover feast. It was imperative that the lamb was without blemish, for it was a type of Christ. Each lamb was inspected before the family could prepare it for the feast. Once a lamb was selected, the family brought it into the home where they would become familiar with the sacrifice. At the right time, they killed the lamb by slitting its throat and placing its blood on the doorpost. The house was now identified with the blood; its inhabitants were safe from the destroyer.

What a perfect picture of Jesus! It was what He was about to go through after He took the cup of redemption, blessed it, and drank it. None of His disciples could fully understand the eternal value of what they were seeing right before their eyes. Chosen as God's pure Lamb, Jesus was about to give up His life to save many from destruction. His blood would become smeared on the doorposts of multitudes to shield them from the destruction. This blood is still activated today.

Coming together as believers in a communion service symbolizes what has taken place in both the spiritual and natural realms. The Lamb of God was slain, and because of His blood we are free from the curse. We are given a new nature and we are bound by something stronger than death itself through the blood of Jesus. Under the new covenant, we can now be a blesser and not curser, just like Jesus was and still is today. I think picking up your cross and following Jesus entails picking up the Cup of Blessing and following in His footsteps. Nothing annoys the devil more than someone who will not take the bait and curse. And we are all called into this celebration of Passover, daily celebrating the life of Christ through blessing those He has blessed.

> *I speak as to wise men; you judge what I say. Is not the **cup** of blessing which we bless a sharing in the blood of Christ? Is not the bread which we break a sharing in the body of Christ?* (1 Corinthians 10:15-16)

A definite yes! The act itself is symbolic of an actuality. By drinking the cup, we are partaking of our covenant through the blood of Jesus. God produces an inward transformation in us where we become people of blessing. He wants to infuse every part of our life with the *eulogia*, so when we speak as a voice for Jesus it affirms the Cross of blessing. Blessing then becomes not just something we use as a greeting but an instrument of power. As freely as we have received blessing, we should as freely give it.

There was one conversation with His disciples where Jesus alluded to the idea of blessing as a lifestyle. What they had wanted were positions and places of authority. What they got was a challenge.

*And He said to her, "What do you wish?" She said to Him, "Command that in Your Kingdom these two sons of mine may sit one on Your right and one on Your left." But Jesus answered, "You do not know what you are asking. **Are you able to drink the cup that I am about to drink?"** They said to Him, "We are able." He said to them, **"My cup you shall drink;** but to sit on My right and on My left, this is not Mine to give, but it is for those for whom it has been prepared by My Father"* (Matthew 20:21-23).

Jesus was referring to His crucifixion when He asked them if they were able to drink the cup He was about to drink. The word "cup" was referring to living out a life of blessing and laying down the life, which at times reverts to cursing.

The Lord's Table was intended to be more than just a Christian ritual. By taking the cup during communion, we are participating in the cup of redemption, which is the Lord's heart to bless. Though the act of communion may be restricted to a time and place, the extension of blessing is not. We could be at home, work, the bus stop, the jungle, in an airplane, in a submarine, you name it, and still bless. Blessing knows no bounds. Every time we bless, we are remembering what Jesus has done. As you extend the cup of blessing, you will see how you are marked for destruction to pass over you.

A promise was made to us during that Passover. Jesus said that He would not drink again of "this" cup until He drank it with us in His Father's Kingdom. At the consummation of the marriage supper of the Lamb (Jesus), we are going to drink of this cup again. He is waiting for us to join Him in this celebration none has ever experienced; until then, we have an engagement. This pledge is best understood in the context of the Jewish culture. When a young Jewish man wanted to marry a girl, he would get permission from her father. If he was permitted to ask her, he took a cup of wine and went to her house. He would extend to her a cup of wine. If she took the wine he, too, would drink. This was to signify her acceptance of his marriage betrothal. We are waiting for His return and the finality of our covenant with Christ. We have drunk the wine and are saying we will be faithful to Him until He returns.

God places great value on the marriage covenant, announcing that what He puts together, no one should separate. He has blessed and betrothed us to His Son with the cup of blessing. He did this through the Cross, and our cup is now full and overflowing. A recap of what is contained in taking the cup is almost mind-blowing: a better covenant, overcoming power, blessing, and a pledge from the Bridegroom Himself—one day, we will drink this cup with Him at that glorious marriage feast. No other celebration since the beginning of creation will compare.

House of Blessing

Mother's voice echoed from the corridors of time: "I plead the blood of Jesus over my family."

Her words rang in my spirit as I studied one night. Those were words that I heard her pray frequently. Little did I realize how powerful that declaration was. I had become so accustomed to hearing it that I dismissed it.

My mother was declaring the cup of blessing. She has gone to her rest and reward, but the power of her words means more to me now than ever before.

The blessing she declared so many years ago continues to have affect. True, the phrase, "pleading the blood" is not in Scripture, but we can find other words that are similar. The word *plead* means, "someone else is making advocacy or pleading another's case." We know that the Holy Spirit is the *parakletos,* or the One who comes alongside us and pleads our case as our advocate (see John 14:26).[2]

Blessing invokes the blood covenant over a house and family. In a similar way, the Israelites placed the blood over their doorposts to keep out death. Sickness and financial disasters cannot stand against the blood of Jesus and the word of our testimony.

When my wife, Diane, and I enter a hotel room (and we've had more than our share of those), she opens the door and says, "I speak the blood of Jesus over this hotel room and sanctify this room as a sanctuary of the Lord and command every unclean spirit out!" I know it works because I don't have any trouble sleeping. When we enter a house let our peace be upon it (see Luke 10:5). If our peace comes back to us, it is like an echo indicating that there is no peace or fellowship/communion there. What if it is our own home that has no peace? Then we go through our house and bless it.

"My peace be upon you! Peace is upon this house!"

The Lord will come and invoke His covenantal right over that home. It is as if He is saying, "I've written My name in this house and nothing deadly will enter." Cursing invalidates the covering, because cursing is in opposition to the work of the Cross and of blessing. Since with blessing comes peace, we can also conclude that with cursing comes the lack of peace and well-being. James tells us not to be *double minded;* a double-minded person is unstable in many ways (see James 1:7-8). Let not the one who is double minded think he will be able to receive anything from the Lord. A double-minded person thinks one way at one moment and another at other times. If you are blessing sometimes and at other times find yourself cursing, then it is possible you may be double minded.

What if we see someone sin? John clarified this. When we see someone sinning that does not lead to death, we are to ask for life. (That means the person is not hardening their heart against God, nor are they blaspheming or denying the will and purpose of God.) We now know that blessing is speaking life and cursing is speaking death. Asking God for life for the one sinning is not agreeing with the sin, it's speaking the intended restoration as to where they should be. The Bible tells us that it is not *God's will that any should perish* but that all should come to the knowledge of Christ (see 2 Peter 3:9).

> *If anyone sees his brother committing a sin not leading to death, he* [those who are seeing] *shall ask and God will for him give life to those who commit sin not leading to death. There is a sin*

leading to death; I do not say that he should make request for this (1 John 5:16).

Condemnation of the sinner may be the natural response, but choosing to bless, we resist being the judge, jury, and executioner. *And so we remain confident that when we pray, our heavenly Father hears us because we have not used our prayer to curse them.*

WITHIN THESE WALLS

I checked the newspaper. My ad was there under the "Used Furniture for Sale." It had been a few days. There had been no calls. We were running out of time for the duration of the ad.

Diane and I decided to bless and not fret. We laid hands on the furniture and began to bless. "I bless this furniture. It is a resource for good to all that will use it. I bless the buyer who will come and buy this furniture; it will be beneficial for them as it has been for us."

Less than an hour later, we received a call from a guy who was interested in looking at the furniture. He wanted to come over right away. I heartily agreed as I prepared myself to negotiate.

The man and his wife arrived soon after and began to check out the furniture. After awhile, the man looked at his wife and asked, "What do you think?"

She was noncommittal. "I don't know."

Now, I had sold furniture before, so I knew they were tire-kickers and were not going to buy it.

Under my breath, I just blessed them: "Lord, I bless them. If they are the blessing of the Lord You sent, thank You. The furniture is worth the price. It is a good deal."

Still bouncing around on the furniture, the guy continued in a conversational tone, "We just moved down here from way up in Seattle. We purchased an airplane and a hanger, and I'm building a little apartment in the hanger. This furniture will work just fine. I'll write you a check for the full price. You can go cash the check first to know that it is good, and I'll come by and pick the furniture up on Monday."

The man never asked me to take a nickel off the price of the furniture. I should note he was the only call we received from our ad.

Since that time, we have not ceased to bless our finances. We have seen supernatural abundance. We have moved from provision to abundance through learning to bless. Redemption and restoration have been poured out in the areas where the enemy has stolen. Complaining and withholding blessing allows the devil to enter the house and steal peace and prosperity. Complaining in many ways is equivalent to charging God that He has not done a very good job of taking care of us.

The Book of Haggai is a good example of what I am discussing.

> *You have sown much, but harvest little; you eat, but there is not enough to be satisfied; you drink, but there is not enough to become drunk; you put on clothing, but no one is warm enough; and he who earns, earns wages to put into a purse with holes* (Haggai 1:6).

No matter how hard they worked, a curse was upon their efforts. The money never lasted long because it was gone as soon as it was earned. The prophet Haggai was sent to speak to those who were focused only on their own houses and lives. They spent time paneling their houses with cedar and left the Temple of God in ruins. Withholding their 10 percent tithe brought a curse on the rest of their produce. When the tithe was given, the other 90 percent was blessed. Ninety percent blessed is greater than a hundred cursed. The Temple was not being rebuilt due to their own self-indulgence. This is a tactic of the enemy, in which he gets us focused solely on our needs and negligent in the purpose of God. One may make more money and yet there is less to show for it, because the whole amount is cursed. Proverbs 16:7 says, *"When a man's ways are pleasing to the Lord, He makes even his enemies to be at peace with him."* Our enemy, the devil, is restrained from stealing peace and prosperity from those whose ways are the ways of the Lord. Tithing is the way of the Lord that breaks the power of poverty. When one gives of the tithe they are saying to the Lord, "I believe You, Lord, and I honor You." God will take what you have and multiply it beyond your ability to earn when it is blessed by honoring the Lord through tithing.

As For Me

God likes being our Protector and Provider. Unless He is the One who captures our hearts as our main Source and Supplier of our life and provision, there will be a vacuum that will be filled by something else. God is the ultimate Blesser; there is no one else that compares.

> *Thus says the Lord,* **"Cursed is the man who trusts in mankind** *and makes flesh his strength, and whose heart turns away from the Lord. For he will be like a bush in the desert and* **will not see when prosperity comes,** *but will live in stony wastes in the wilderness, a land of salt without inhabitant"* (Jeremiah 17:5-6).

Another side of the curse is being blinded to God's ways. Then it becomes like the story of the man who waited on his rooftop for God to rescue him from the flood. Turning down the boat and then the helicopter that came by to save him, he kept waiting for God's rescue squad. Finally, he died, drowned by the rising waters. Help had come, but his idea of what the Lord's help looked like did not match with reality. He did not see when good came.

I can truly tell you that part of the blessing of the Lord is being able to see opportunities when they are sent your way. One who is living under a curse feels as if nothing good ever comes their way and everybody else has the opportunities. They are blinded due to the curse.

God sent the prophet to the widow whose family was facing bankruptcy and slavery to pay off their debts (see 2 Kings 4:3-4). In her eyes, she had nothing of worth to keep her family alive. What she did have she made available to the prophet for multiplying. She obeyed the Word of the Lord and poured what little she had into *other vessels* and the oil continued to increase as long as she had *other vessels* to pour into.

One who is constantly cursing those who are more successful usually feels victimized by society. They tend to feel they have an entitlement to what others have. The only way to break this cycle of cursing is to start blessing and speaking over others what you would like to inherit for yourself. Blessing will break the generational cycle of cursing over your life.

> **Blessed is the man who trusts in the Lord** *and whose trust is the Lord. For he will be like a tree planted by the water, that extends its roots by a stream and will not fear when the heat comes; but its leaves will be green, and it will not be anxious in a year of drought nor cease to yield fruit* (Jeremiah 17:7-8).

Notice the contrast between these two verses and the two before them. One refers to the curse on those who only trust in mankind, and the other is blessed when he trusts in the Lord. It's the picture of a tree. Not just any tree, but a strong and secure tree with roots dug deep near the water source. So let the heat and drought come! Let the wind blow! With roots firmly planted and absorbing life, they are not moved. Fear and anxiety are not driving them to the wrong sources. Security for them comes from God's presence and their association to the River of Life.

Satisfied in the Lord and their relationship to Him, they are alerted to pending times ahead. Can you see how worry is not even a factor? Yes, they are happy! Why not? There could be a drought going on, but their leaves are green and they are bearing fruit! Others benefit from your blessed life. Remember, that was the promise to Abraham—that he would not only be blessed but that he would be a blessing to all the families of the earth. Maybe you are to be the first one in your family to break out of the cycle and start blessing and becoming a tree planted by the River of Life. Begin the day with blessing and end it with the same. We all need the power of blessing. Remember the old adage that says to keep doing the same things and expecting different results is insanity? Well, cursing is insane.

PRAYER

Father, I release conviction in our hearts and a commitment that we are going to be a house of blessing and a people of blessing. We resolve to speak those things that we have need of and sow them in righteousness and faith to our children and the next generation. As Proverbs says, our children will rise up and call us blessed.

Father, we present ourselves to You as living sacrifices. We want to be holy and acceptable. Let the words our mouths and the meditations of our hearts be acceptable in Your sight. Forgive us, O God, for our coarse joking and brutal or idle conversations that tear down without building up. Cause us to extend Your cup of blessing to those around us from this point forward.

TYPICAL HOUSE BLESSING
(Pray this over your house.)

This is the house of the Lord. It is Bethel; it is a place of blessing. The peace of God rules and reigns here. No unclean spirit shall be able to have place here. I cast out every spirit of strife, division, and discord. I cast out the spirit of poverty. I invoke the blessing of the Lord that makes rich and adds no sorrow. I release the presence of the Lord upon my husband, my wife, and upon my children. My children shall be taught of the Lord and great peace shall be upon them. No weapon formed against us shall prosper (see Isa. 54:17). Every voice raised in judgment shall be found to be false, for this is the heritage of the children of the Lord.

ENDNOTES

1. Biblesoft's New Exhaustive Strong's Numbers and Concordance with Expanded Greek-Hebrew Dictionary. CD-ROM. Biblesoft, Inc. and International Bible Translators, Inc., *eulogia* (5117).

2. Strong's, *parakletos* (3875).

Chapter Eleven

Tribe of Blessing

"Who's Your Daddy?"

My daily routine included a trip to Moore's Fine Food. It was the highlight of my day. Of course, I was only about eight years old. Times were much simpler then. I would ride my bike about a mile from our house to school on days when the weather permitted. Near Pleasant Valley School was the grocery store. It was a treat for me to eat in the cafeteria at school. The lunch cost thirty cents and four cents for milk. There were no credit cards to speak of except gasoline cards. My Dad had arranged for me to get my lunch money from the grocer, Mr. Moore. I was allowed the thirty cents for lunch and a dime's worth of candy after school on the way home.

My friend Dave came with me one afternoon and he saw me get my ration of candy and sign a ticket without any money. Dave thought that was easy enough, so he got his stash and laid it upon the counter. Mr. Moore asked for the money. Dave politely said, "I will do what Kerry does and spell my name."

Mr. Moore replied, "I know his daddy, but I don't know your father." My father's name was good there because he was trusted to pay the bill on time each month.

Wow, what a lesson for an eight-year-old! I realized that the family name was a real benefit under certain circumstances. My dad's name was worth something, and I was treated in a manner of respect that was relative to my family name. It was comforting to know that when I would sign my dad's name, I had authority to ask without any fear of rejection.

Understanding our heritage in our heavenly Father is the confidence we have that, *"if we ask anything according to His will, He hears us"* (1 John 5:14). I was blessed greatly because my father had a good name. My being blessed was directly related to the family name. Proverbs 22:1 says, *"A good name is to be more desired than great wealth, favor is better than silver and gold."*

The family name was very important in the Jewish culture during the time Jesus was teaching His disciples about the Kingdom of God. In the Scriptures, many times a man would be introduced as "the son of." For instance, David was called the son of Jesse. Their identity was understood by who their father was.

Since Jesus was not conceived through an earthly father, His DNA was not from an earthly identity, though He grew up in an earthly family. His followers had difficulty understanding why He would say, *"I only do what I see my Father do"* (see John 5:19-20).

When He was about 12 years old, He stayed behind and debated with the religious leaders in the synagogue while his family returned home. When His mother discovered He was not with them, they searched and found Him at the Temple. When asked why He was not with them, He replied, *"I must be about My Father's business"* (Luke 2:49 NKJV).

Even at this young age, Jesus was identifying who His Father was. The more Jesus would refer to His Father, the more curious His followers were as to who His Father was. This was unusual for them because their foundation of thinking was earthly, and a person's authority was held to the level of their family name and status.

Jesus begins to tell them about His Father's house and the many places that were there. He said:

> *Do not let your heart be troubled; believe in God, believe also in Me. In My Father's house are many dwelling places; if it were not so I would have told you; for I go and prepare a place for you. If I go to prepare a place for you, I will come again and receive you to Myself, that where I am, there you may be also* (John 14:1-3).

Thomas could stand it no longer. He blurted out the question the others wanted to ask but feared to.

> *Thomas said to Him, "Lord, we do not know where You are going, how do we know the way?" Jesus said to him, "I am the way, and the truth, and the life; no one comes to the Father but through Me"* (John 14:5-6).

Thomas' question may not seem too important to us in western culture, but for a Jew is was paramount. Thomas was implying, "If we are going to follow You, then tell us where You came from and who Your Father is so we can know where we are going." In Middle Eastern culture, your father's identity and status defined your future. If they could grasp who His Father was, they could finally know the way and their destination.

> *Philip said to Him, "Lord, **show us the Father**, and it is enough for us." Jesus said to him, "Have I been so long with you, and yet you have not come to know Me, Philip? **He who has seen Me has seen the Father**; how can you say, 'Show us the Father?'"* (John 14:8-9)

Why was it important for Philip to know the Father? For a Jew, knowing someone's father said plenty about the man himself, for it revealed his identity and DNA. Jewish people understood the strong connection between the father and the family place. First names did not have as much identity as one's father or place of origin.

Revealing the father showed the identity of the son. The disciples wanted a clear picture of Jesus' Father so they would know what awaited them. Such knowledge in Middle Eastern culture determined one's level of expectation. If the groom's father was not a man of means, then the place he was going to prepare could be out in the wilderness somewhere or in a poverty-stricken area. But if the father was a man of means, the expectation as to a new couple's future was heightened.

Now this is where the connection to believers everywhere comes in. Essentially, when Jesus was saying He was going to build a place for His Bride that was a form of covenant agreement. Knowing where we come from spiritually is essential, for it speaks of our eternal destiny. Our new-birth experience grafted us into our heavenly Father. No matter what family we are born into, when we are born again we have new DNA from our new birth Father. By revelation, we come to know that our heavenly Father is not poor, nor is He abusive.

Jesus wants us to know the Father and to know He is the Father of blessing. Our new family identity is one of blessing. This heavenly family's identity is known by its character of blessing. The Holy Spirit is the Tutor of the family. He will guide us to be like our Father. The attribute of our Father is blessing. As sons and daughters, we learn that the family DNA is to bless and not curse. The greater the revelation we have of our Father in Heaven, the greater the confidence we have when we pray. Those who bless have a much easier time in prayer than those who are more prone to have a negative outlook. Their prayers tend to focus more on rehearsing the problem before the Lord than announcing the solution through blessing.

Jesus restored us to the Father through His adoption. We are no longer slaves to a cursed life, but we have a life of fullness and blessing. Many want the benefits of knowing the Father without being part of His family. His family members have certain protocols that mark them as belonging to Him. The blessed life of one who has been translated out of the kingdom of darkness into the Kingdom of God carries a reservoir of blessing waiting to be released upon others.

I have taken men much older than I through a kind of spiritual Bar Mitzvah. When they experienced the Father blessing them as a son it was amazing the change that took place. There is an old adage that goes something like this: "You are never a man until your father says you are." A Bar Mitzvah (or a Bat Mitzvah for girls) in Jewish culture is the celebration and commissioning for young men that gives them the rights of passage into being an adult. The Bar Mitzvah gave the young man the right to conduct business in the family name. The responsibility of not dishonoring the family also came with this privilege. The father of a young man or girl would place his hands on them and give them a blessing. The blessing would include declarations about prosperity and long life. It was a prophetic guide to their destiny.

I believe with all my being that God honors these kinds of blessings over our children. Sure they have choices in all they do. Proverbs tells us to *train up a child in the way he should go; even when he is old he will not depart from it* (Prov. 22:6). Blessing is a prophetic blueprint set into their spirit, and they will not forget that moment of passage. *The blessing of a father is a powerful act given to us by God. It will connect the hearts of your children to you like nothing else can. To know their father approves of them is a tool in the development of their life.*

There may be those who have fears resulting from painful relationships with their fathers. They are concerned that they will repeat the same with their children. If this is you, you can be free today by receiving the blessing from your heavenly Father. He has good things to declare over your life. This will give you confidence that you can conduct the family business using the name of your heavenly Father. You no longer have to feel helpless, repeating the old patterns that have plagued your family for generations. Welcome to the family of blessing.

When we become Christians, we enter a whole new paradigm for living. We cannot continue to blame our biological or adoptive parents for our actions anymore. Our heavenly Father waits for us to grow up into His image and live out of His declared blessing over us.

There is a need for proper maturity in the area of spiritual gifting. The gifts of God are free, but maturity is costly. Though we are promised gifts at a young age, we have to come to maturity. God does not withhold them from us; rather, He waits for the proper time—when we come of age. Are we ready for the responsibilities that come with that gift? We have to grow up into Him first. Eventually, the Father will release for us what He promised and begin to do the family business.

THE FULLNESS OF TIME

...As long as the heir is a child he does not differ at all from a slave although he is owner of everything, but he is under guardians and managers until the date set by the father (Galatians 4:1-2).

This verse is referring to Jesus who, when he was a child, was still under authority though he was heir of all creation. Notice He continues to be under guardians until the time when the Father releases Him. Part of the tutorial of maturing for those growing up in the family of God is to learn to bless and not curse or dishonor the Lord's name.

Jesus did not show Phillip a personal testimony when He was asked to show the Father. He showed them a life committed to finish and go the distance, even to the Cross—a life of distinction that will stand out. Before long, you learn to practice being a blesser; the line is fairly distinct between those who practice cursing as part of the fallen nature of Adam and those who bless after the resurrected Second Adam.

One side of my family stood on the side of blessing and the other side stood for cursing. The side that stood for blessing has prospered and their families live in peace. I cannot say the same for the side who indulged in cursing. Some of them died prematurely, some were captured by drug addictions and spent time in prison. Our future is tied to which side of life we stand on.

TWO MOUNTAINS

When it came time for Israel to cross the Jordan and claim their inheritance, God told Moses to divide the 12 tribes. Six of the tribes stood on Mount Gerizim and the other six tribes on Mount Ebal. The tribes were specifically selected for which mountain each would stand on (see Deut. 27:11-13). Mount Gerizim was to be the mountain of blessing and Mount Ebal was to be the place for cursing. They were to rehearse the blessings and the curses before they could enter the land. God wanted them to know how to live in the land and prosper through blessing, but if they chose cursing then the land would not be favorable to them. One by one, the blessings and the curses were read out loud and the congregation of Israel would agree. Here is a glance at the list of where each tribe was positioned.

BLESSING	CURSING
Simeon	Reuben
Levi	Gad
Judah	Asher
Issachar	Zebulun
Joseph	Dan
Benjamin	Naphtali

Travel with these tribes throughout Scripture, and it becomes clear why God chose which tribe to represent either blessing or cursing on those mountains. Levi, the tribe of the priesthood, brought the Israelites before God and represented Him on the earth. To be a priest required that one be born a Levite. Their job was to perform the sacrifices and make atonement for the people. Blessings followed wherever the Levites functioned properly in their God-given place.

Joseph was also on the mountain of blessing. He was *"a fruitful bough, a fruitful bough by a spring; its branches run over a wall"* (Gen. 49:22). He was the one who was strategically placed in Egypt to deliver his family from a prolonged and extensive time of famine. Captivity was how Joseph ended up in Egypt, but God exalted him there and brought deliverance from death for the other 11 tribes. And that was just two of the six tribes who were on the mountain of blessing.

God will place people in our lives or position us so that at the right time and place, while doing the right thing, deliverance will come to someone else. Joseph did not fully understand how he ended up in the pit and prison in Egypt—not until later. Usually, the reason for being strategically placed somewhere is veiled at first and unfolds with time.

TRIBE OF JUDAH

Standing on the mountain of blessing was also the tribe of Judah. The Lord set His love and wrote His name on Judah—an honor that other tribes were not given.

> *He also rejected the tent of Joseph, and did not choose the tribe of Ephraim, but **chose the tribe of Judah,** Mount Zion **which He loved*** (Psalms 78:67-68).

Judah was known for several characteristics. One of those was being a tribe that blessed God and people. King David, the Psalmist and the man after God's own heart, was born into the tribe of Judah. David's deep reliance on and love for God is recorded in the book of Psalms. The Lord assured the throne to David's descendants as long as they obeyed the covenant (see Ps. 132:11-12). But a descendant of David to whom the throne belonged to forever was foretold even from the beginning of the tribe of Judah. He would bring blessing and hope to the world.

The scepter shall not depart from Judah, nor the ruler's staff from between his feet, until Shiloh comes, and to him shall be the obedience of the peoples (Genesis 49:10).

That scepter means "authority." Though kings and rulers came from Judah, in time, Shiloh (Jesus) did come and fulfilled this word (see Luke 1:32). Jesus became the ultimate Blesser who gave His life to redeem all of humankind and restore them to God. Called the Lion of Judah, Jesus became a sacrificial Lamb that paid the ransom price so we could stand on the mountain of blessing. He made it possible for the rest of the world to be included in God's promises of blessing that were given to His chosen people, the Israelites.

Not only was Judah a tribe that blessed, it was also an overcomer.

I will bring forth offspring from Jacob, and an heir of My mountains from Judah; even My chosen ones shall inherit it, and My servants will dwell there (Isaiah 65:9).

Even as they settled the Promised Land, the tribe of Judah ruled over its enemies. Its borders in the Promised Land encompassed mountain areas where Judah settled (see Josh. 15:8-11). Mountains are the ideal place from which to rule one's enemies. Keeping an eye on the enemy is easier from the mountaintop than if one was down in the valley. Notice how God gave Judah detailed, strategic positioning.

Judah is translated "praise." True to the name, Judah was a tribe that was known for honor and praise. Judah shall ever be praising before the throne of God. Not to belabor a point made earlier, but praise plows the hard ground in preparation for harvest.

Judah shall plow; Jacob shall break his clods (Hosea 10:11 NKJV).

While Judah plowed through praise, the 11 tribes followed behind breaking up the clods. Judah was destined to lead in instructing. God promised to inhabit the praise of His people (see Ps. 22:3). In the midst of the congregation, the

Lord would sit as they worshiped Him. He was present wherever His people praised Him, and wherever He was, there was blessing. This is a forever truth that we as believers in Christ enjoy today.

> *God is known in Judah; His name is great in Israel. His* **tabernacle** *is in Salem* [Jerusalem]; *His dwelling place also is in* **Zion** (Psalm 76:1-2).

God's tabernacle is His presence. Judah is equated with Zion, the city of the great king. It is a city that draws the eyes of the world in beauty and significance.

> *Beautiful in elevation, the joy of the whole earth, is Mount Zion on* **the sides of the north,** *the city of the great King* (Psalm 48:2 NKJV).

The "sides of the north" here refer to the Church in Scripture. It was the place where lucifer wanted to position himself to receive worship.

> *For you have said in your heart: "I will ascend into Heaven, I will exalt my throne above the stars of God; I will also sit on the mount of the congregation on the farthest* **sides of the north"** (Isaiah 14:13 NKJV).

But that place was not for him. Remember what happened to the devil? (We discussed it in Chapter Nine.) That place belongs to Jesus Christ alone, the Head of the Church. So satan continues to salivate for something that he will never possess.

YOU ARE HERE

Hebrews says it best:

> *For when the priesthood is changed, of necessity there takes place a change of law also. For the one concerning whom these*

things are spoken belongs to another tribe, from which no one has officiated at the altar. For it is evident that our Lord was descended from Judah, a tribe with reference to which Moses spoke nothing concerning priests (Hebrews 7:12-14).

Where we fit into this big picture is the most exciting part for me. *Every believer that enters into the Kingdom of God under the new covenant gets grafted into the tribe of Judah.* We can say that blessing is the DNA of Judah. God placed Judah on the mountain of blessing with the prophetic picture that Jesus the Messiah would come out of the tribe of blessing. We are placed into the lineage of the *Tribe of Blessing.* Wouldn't you say that is enough cause for a celebration?

Jesus Christ made this possible by grafting us in through His death and resurrection. Once we were wild branches and outsiders, but now we are grafted in to become part of God's people (see Rom. 11:17). But the blessings God had spoken over Abraham concerning his natural descendants, the Jews, and the grafted-in ones remain. The Jews are still blessed because God's Word cannot be annulled. Even when the Jews take a different route, God has set upon them certain blessings and words that no one can eradicate, not even the United States or any other nation. Paul the apostle did argue this point thoroughly in several places in the New Testament.

> *I say then, God has not rejected His people, has He? May it never be! For I too am an Israelite, a descendant of Abraham, of the tribe of Benjamin* (Romans 11:1).

Some who have replaced God's promise to the Jews—called replacement theology—with the Church are misinformed. God does not disown those who He has made a covenant with.

> *I say then, they did not stumble so as to fall, did they? May it never be! But by their transgression salvation has come to the Gentiles, to make them jealous. **Now if their transgression is riches for the world and their failure is riches for the Gentiles,***

*how much more will their fulfillment be! …Inasmuch then as I am an apostle of Gentiles, I magnify my ministry, if somehow I might move to jealousy my fellow countrymen and save some of them. For **if their rejection is the reconciliation of the world, what will their acceptance be but life from the dead*** (Romans 11:11-15).

We are benefiting from the Jews' rejection. As believers, we are tapping into the blessing of Abraham through Jesus Christ. By witnessing the blessing and peace upon the followers of Jesus Christ, Jews would be curious and even jealous of it enough to make them want it (see Rom. 10:19). Today, a large number of Jews are coming to faith and receiving Jesus the Christ as their Messiah.

And there's more. The tribe of Levi was exclusively the order of the priesthood. That role did not mix with the position of ruling…not until Jesus Christ came. The Lord Jesus Christ is not only a King but also a Priest. We, as His followers, are given the same honor and privilege of being kings and priests with Jesus (see Rev. 1:5-6). So, through the tribe of Judah, we have come into the priesthood as a new order. This revelation can cause one to change sides of the mountain and start blessing.

*Gilead is Mine; Manasseh is Mine; Ephraim also is the helmet for My head; **Judah is My lawgiver*** (Psalms 108:8 NKJV).

God is concerned about every area of our lives. He cares about those who rule and those who are ruled. In the end, justice is going to flow out of Judah. If we want justice, we bless people in authority, including judges, policemen, and so on. Opportunities arise daily for us to practice this tribal right to bless, like my recent encounter with a police officer.

While driving back from Houston, Texas, I was busy talking on my cell phone when a state trooper pulled me over.

Having now understood the importance of blessing, my wife and I began to bless that officer as we pulled the vehicle to a stop. I knew I had not been speeding at that moment. The trooper came up to my truck and stated, "You don't have a license plate on the front of your truck."

I replied, "Yes sir. I brought this truck out of Louisiana."

"Well, in Texas we are a two-tag state."

I was apologetic. "OK, I did not know that."

"Where are you coming from?"

"Houston."

"What were you doing down there?"

"I was ministering in a seminar to pastors," I responded enthusiastically.

He took a quick glance at me and then asked, "Well, how did it go?"

I beamed, "Very well." He gave me a warning and went back to his car. My wife and I continued to speak blessings over him as he left. There is no guarantee that blessing the police will get you out of a ticket, but it does help the attitude toward those in authority. After all, we are of the Tribe of Blessing.

Being part of the Tribe of Blessing brings favor. For example, a member of my church had bought some land in a good location with the intentions to build multiple-family dwellings. He talked to the city and got the preliminary release to start building. He poured the slabs and began framing. Then he learned that the city was not going to bring the utilities to the property. They still refused, even though he was far enough along that he could not stop. After much debate about why they had given the initial permits to start construction and then refuse city services, it seemed they were at an impasse.

Frustrated as he was, he decided to try blessing the people who were in charge. After seeding the situation with blessing, he was determined to try again. This time, they acted as if no one had even said no to him. He said it was strange because they could not understand why he was turned down in the first place. He attributes this 180-degree switch to the favor that comes with blessing.

Are you plowing through some hard ground lately with family members or those who are in authority? Consider how you would like for someone to bless you, and then declare that same blessing over those you are in opposition with.

> *For rulers are not a cause for fear for good behavior, but for evil...* (Romans 13:3).

> *...For there is no authority except from God, and those which exist are established by God* (Romans 13:1).

When the apostle Paul wrote this, the Roman occupation was still in control of the Hebrew nation. It seems difficult at times to be able to bless those in authority that are cruel and unmerciful. But honoring and blessing those who don't deserve blessing is not the issue. It is all about honoring the Lord who has honored their position of leadership. Though all authority is of God, not all leaders and rulers behave in a godly manner. Remember, blessing is not about the circumstances at the moment. However, by declaring God's intentions it releases the prophetic potential for something to change.

PRAYER

Father, I thank You for the power of Christ that operates in and through us.

We stand in the family name and a Christ-given name by the Spirit of the Lord. We choose to stand on the mountain of blessing. We stand to bless and speak over our nation and families, declaring on earth that the United States of America is a nation under God. We bless the president, the cabinet, and those of various political affiliations. We thank You, God, for the power of grace that operates through the Tribe of Blessing.

We refuse to live on the mountain of cursing. We defeat every curse with a blessing. We thank You, Lord, that we have been grafted in, born of the spirit of Christ and born into the Tribe of Blessing.

CHAPTER TWELVE

---◆---

NOBODY SAW IT

Blessing is a means to confront issues in our life that are weaknesses. Many of us have things we try to go around instead of overcoming. Four times in Revelation 2, the term *overcoming* is used. For instance, in Revelation 2:7 it says, *"To him who overcomes, I will grant to eat of the Tree of Life which is in the Paradise of God."*

"To overcome" is the opposite of "to endure" or "to undergo." There is great reward for those who overcome. It is God's way of introducing and increasing authority and maturity in our life. In the times of the kings in Middle Eastern culture, kings would go to war over territory and superiority. Gaining wealth and spoil was done through conquest against a rival king. When a king would conquer a city or another king, he would ride through the streets placing the crown of the defeated king on his own head, declaring there was a new sheriff in town. This was a show of gaining authority by overcoming an enemy. In Revelation, there is the account of those casting their crowns (plural) before the throne of God. This is purely my supposition here, but I wonder—where did they get these crowns? Could it be the conquests they won and the subsequent crowns from those victories? When individuals overcome an addiction, I believe they gain authority over the enemy.

Instead of using creative means to avoid confrontation with our weaknesses, why not overcome and gain new freedom along with greater authority? Blessing your mind to have the mind of Christ so you can overcome is a start. We have talked at length about blessing others; we should also look at blessing ourselves. Declare over yourself that you are a child of God who lacks for nothing and will see good days in the land of the living. Blessing what is weak in you through speaking God's intentions will provide opportunities to get free. That blockage is not there to keep you from success, it is there as an opportunity for conquest to gain the spoil.

I had a similar opportunity that I was trying to avoid like the plague. It was funeral services. It was not in my list of things I like to attend or do as a young pastor just starting out in ministry, mainly because of my inexperience. When I started the church I thought I had an agreement with God that I would do anything He asked me to do if I could only get out of doing funerals. I was spooked about death as a kid. My older siblings saw to it that I heard plenty of their taunting about dead bodies and being buried alive. You know, the childish pranks we grow up fearing; the stuff of too many Alfred Hitchcock thrillers.

After being in my first pastorate in eastern Texas for a few months, I guess it was bound to happen. God was setting me up to confront my phobia. I was asked to do a funeral. Having never officiated at a funeral before (I had done a eulogy once) and being the new guy in town, I was somewhat nervous. My dislike for funeral services added to that discomfort. (I had attended a funeral for the first time in my twenties.) To complicate matters, I hardly knew the family and had never seen the deceased person before. Keenly aware of how people watched everything that I did because I was new, I wanted to do a good job. Thankfully, the service at the chapel went well and I was greatly relieved.

Soon, the time came when we had to travel to the gravesite. As the officiating pastor, it was customary for me to ride with the funeral director in the lead car. The problem was that the lead car was the hearse. Not only was I uncomfortable dealing with the dead, but now I was locked in a moving vehicle hauling a dead body. How I wished I could ride in any other vehicle but the hearse!

"O God," I thought, "What if You decide to raise this guy behind me today?" I consoled myself with the thought that I would surely make a new door. As we drove along, the funeral director asked me if I had done a country funeral before.

"Man, I have never done a city funeral before, much less a country one," I replied. "I don't have a particular way of doing it one way or another. What do I do?"

He explained, "The only thing about a country funeral is that at the end of the graveside service, you take your boutonnière off and place it on the lid of the casket. You step away from it, and that is how we know that the service is over. Then the pall bearers will follow the same." It sounded simple, a no-brainer.

"Hey, I can handle that," I said. When we arrived at the cemetery, the funeral director cautioned, "By the way, do be careful because this is a country cemetery and we have to carry the casket in for probably about seventy-five or a hundred yards."

I thought that was OK, because I was not one of the pall bearers; they were doing the heavy lifting. Feeling somewhat relieved because everything was going as planned, I proceeded to take my place at the head of the gravesite with the casket in place. After waxing eloquent using Corinthians 15 as my text for the final interment, I was coming in for the landing. I could see the end in sight.

Suddenly, I realized that my boutonnière was not going to stay on the smoothly curved top of the casket. Should my boutonnière fall off when I placed it on the coffin, there was no telling what that would do to the family. I know it sounds strange, but I did not want to be the one who caused any more grief to the family with a falling boutonnière.

Quickly I figured out (with the engineering mind that I have) that if I could get my boutonnière close to the big spray of flowers positioned in the middle of the casket it would stick. People still had their heads bowed and eyes closed, while I rambled on in prayer, praying like a Pharisee as I pushed my boutonnière ever so close to connect with the end of that spray. I was pushing until I was within about four or five inches before I ran out of arm reach.

Suddenly, something happened. I thought we had had an earthquake, because the ground opened up below me and swallowed me up, and I was staring at the bottom of the grave. The ground close to the edge of the grave was sandy and it caved in, leaving me suspended with one elbow leaning on the bier (which holds the casket over the grave) the other one holding onto what little ground was left intact. It was in the heat of the summer and I was in a three-piece polyester suit, the dress of the day! And there I hung, hot and dusty, while bouncing, dangling, and flailing, wondering—*How am going to get out of this?*

All this time I was still praying the closing prayer, knowing that if I stopped praying, everyone would open their eyes and see the fiasco. After what seemed like an eternity and several attempts to get out, I got one leg up behind me and pushed up (being in much better shape in those days). I was able to lift myself up and out of the hole.

I stepped back behind the casket and said, "Amen." The funeral director came over to me and said, "Pastor, I saw what was going on, but I did not know what to do because I was trained not to interrupt while prayer is going on. But I must commend you for a good recovery."

Thinking that I had blown this special time for this family, I felt very bad. But there was nothing I could do to change it because the people were coming by to greet me. They were genuinely grateful and said kind things. None said anything about what had happened. It soon became apparent to me that not a single person had seen that I had fallen in, except for the funeral director.

In my heart I asked the Lord, "Oh God, is it always going to be this hard?"

And I heard Him say to me, "As long as you will walk with Me, I will cover you in times of your vulnerability."

UNCOVERED

Elusive success, unfulfilled promises, and dashed hopes seem to be their lot in life. These are the negative patterns that function in some of the lives that I occasionally come across. More often than not, something happens that sabotages their expectations. As a result, they back off and are reluctant to believe for anything anymore. Lowered expectations become the protection against such disappointments.

Whatever causes expected goodness to be sabotaged? I believe these are rooted in the issues of covering and love. Obviously, not every negative happening that comes our way is related to being under a curse. Sometimes bad decisions have a way of making us feel cursed. I am not referring to those kinds of issues. There are some who cannot find any relief or favor in their life. I am not one who blames the devil for every disappointment in life. I do believe there are people who may not be aware of generational oppression that comes by a curse.

Like a sparrow in its flitting, like a swallow in its flying, so a curse without a cause does not alight (Proverbs 26:2).

Remember my definition for a curse: to place something in a lower position than what God intended. It is safe to say that one does not come under a curse casually or easily. For one who is a born-again believer, a curse must have a cause to have any affect. Someone cursing you is not enough; there would need to be a point of acceptance through an open door. That pathway could be agreement by also cursing others, or maybe through fear that curse has power over you.

There are curses that come due to family members—such as a father or grandfather—being part of cultic groups who take oaths against their own bodies and their children's children. For instance, Freemasonry uses degrees of oaths that may appear harmless on the surface, but when you read the oaths that affect their posterity they are anything but harmless. These oaths are not usually known by the family members, so it would be important to learn if you have had any close relatives involved in Freemasonry. For more information about Freemasonry and its effects on families, go to www.jubilee.org.nz and follow the link for prayers. I have witnessed firsthand the freedom and increased favor when the cursing of Freemasonry is reversed through blessing.

A FATHER'S CURSE

Walk with me through a biblical account of a family where the issue of covering affected the generations that followed.

> Then **Noah** *began farming and planted a vineyard. He drank of the wine and became drunk, and* **uncovered himself** *inside his tent.* **Ham,** *the father of Canaan,* **saw the nakedness of his father, and told his two brothers outside.** *But* **Shem and Japheth took a garment** *and laid it upon both their shoulders and walked backward* **and covered the nakedness of their father; and their faces were turned away, so that they did not see their father's nakedness** (Genesis 9:20-23).

Noah began to rebuild life on the earth. He made a vineyard—also another first recorded in the Bible. Enjoying the fruit was satisfying until Noah had too much wine and passed out in his tent, naked. Along came Ham and saw his father exposed. Unaware that he was setting in motion unfortunate consequences for his lineage, Ham further exposed his father by telling his two brothers. His brothers did the honorable thing and covered their father's nakedness immediately. No one else needed to witness Noah in his vulnerable moment.

When sobered, Noah discovered what Ham had done, and Noah cursed Canaan, the son of Ham, by saying, *"Cursed be Canaan; a servant of servants he shall be to his brothers"* (Gen. 9:25). Notice it was Ham's son that received the curse, and the curse placed him lower than even a servant to serve his brothers. Noah blessed the two brothers for their honor in covering their father by saying:

Blessed be the Lord, the God of Shem; and let Canaan be his servant. May God enlarge Japheth, and let him dwell in the tents of Shem; and let Canaan be his servant (Genesis 9:26-27).

Uncovering someone is a serious matter in the eyes of God. Ham's sin was not in witnessing his father's nakedness but in telling of what he saw. He could have easily covered his father's nakedness just as his brothers did when they found out. Ham also violated a spiritual principle. Belittling a parent, dignitary, or anyone that is in a place of authority by making them appear foolish or look silly places those doing the mocking in a lowered position. Ham was belittling and making Noah appear lower than what God intended him to be.

Those doing the cursing may not realize that they are placing themselves in the place of the cursed. Remember, Jesus came to deliver and defend those who are under a curse. Someone deliberately cursing for sport will find themselves in opposition to the Cross. Ham's action placed him in a cursed position and brought a curse on his lineage. The cause that brought a curse to Ham's family was his own dishonoring of the one who had authority over his life.

So when is the telling of something gossip and when is it not? Gossip's sting is to expose someone for the purpose of turning the hearts of others away from them. One cannot be accused of gossip if they choose to bless as a way to turn the situation for good. If their desire is to turn the situation for something other than good, then the motive could not be from a heart of blessing. Informing someone who then has the ability and authority to help the situation for the good—this is different.

If anyone sees his brother committing a sin not leading to death, he shall ask and God will for him give life... (1 John 5:16).

John encourages us to ask God on behalf of the one going astray rather than tell others of their failures. Choices we make as fathers will open or close the doors to cursing. A father walking before the Lord in a righteous way releases the blessing of the Lord to the third and fourth generation. If a father is cursed we will find it passed down, as in the case with Cain (see Exod. 20:5). Turning to the Lord, however, reverses the curse and establishes the favor of the Lord.

There is a strong thread throughout Scripture about the necessity of having mentors and spiritual fathers in our lives. Having godly mentors and spiritual fathers can produce a healthy and proper perspective of authority.

Remember, the brothers who covered their father Noah were not only blessed, but so were their offspring for generations to come. Neither they nor their brother Ham ever imagined that their acts of covering or uncovering would lead to such drastic effects that would change their families for generations. Notice, the curser became the cursed and the blesser became the blessed. The one who covered and ultimately was blessed was also the one who became master to the one who did the uncovering or cursing.

In the following chapter, we are briefly introduced to Nimrod, a grandson of Ham and someone whom the Bible called a *"mighty hunter before the Lord"* (Gen. 10:9). Nimrod built Babel. Does that sound familiar? Shinar was the whole Babylonian empire; today, we would call it Iraq, Iran, and some of Saudi Arabia.

All the other sons of Noah inhabited the other parts of the Middle East, Canaan, and Gaza. They were shepherds. There is a great difference between the heart of a shepherd and that of a hunter. A shepherd is one with a caring heart. David and Jesus are both referred to as shepherds. David was an actual shepherd and Jesus was the spiritual Shepherd of those lost through sin. A hunter stalks his prey through craftiness and camouflage. The contrast between these three brothers is worth noting. Their lives took on different perspectives and natures after the event of covering—or in Ham's case uncovering—their father's nakedness, which brought on a blessing—or a curse.

Let's revisit a heavenly event where lucifer, an angel made to be a covering, became one that uncovers. It was the first act of rebellion against authority.

> *You were in Eden, the garden of God;* ***every precious stone was*** ***your covering:*** *the ruby, the topaz and the diamond; the beryl, the onyx and the jasper; the lapis lazuli, the turquoise and the*

*emerald; and the gold, the workmanship of your settings and sockets, was in you. On the day that you were created they were prepared. You were **the anointed cherub who covers,** and I placed you there. You were on the holy mountain of God; you walked in the midst of the stones of fire. You were blameless in your ways from the day you were created **until unrighteousness was found in you.** By the abundance of your trade you were internally filled with violence, and you sinned; therefore I have cast you as profane from the mountain of God. And I have destroyed you, O **covering cherub,** from the midst of the stones of fire* (Ezekiel 28:13-16).

Lucifer was the angel created to oversee the sights and sounds of Heaven. In-built with gems and instruments, he was literally a beautiful walking orchestra! Few angels were privileged to enter the throne room of God, and lucifer was one of them. His job was to cover and release the presence of God and lead the angelic hosts in the worship of God. But something dark lurked in the recesses of his heart that corrupted him. Lucifer wanted to be the one that was worshiped. Eventually, that led him to conspire and with a third of the angels, he made war against God the Creator Himself. That day, he moved from being a covering cherub to being an uncovering one. Exposing and uncovering the saints before the Lord became his new specialty. The fallen angel had become the devil and the *"accuser* [or curser] *of the brethren."*

Yet God, who is all about covering and blessing, sent us the One who truly covers—His Son Jesus Christ. Jesus' shed blood became the covering and cleansing from sin. Jesus' blood, placed upon the Mercy Seat in Heaven, not only covered us but cleansed us. The devil will do anything to introduce us to cursing. Working against a relationship, the enemy attempts to weaken those ties by tempting us to uncover each other. Everyone will need the covering grace of God at some point in life.

HUSBANDS, LOVE YOUR WIVES

Nothing covers like love. I am referring to the kind of love that covers a multitude of sins—the *agape* kind of love. This kind of love is a spirit, because the Bible tells us that God is love and that God is Spirit. Without God's kind of love in the earth, there would be anarchy to the point that there would be no restraint or self-control of any kind. Humankind left alone is destructive and very self-indulgent. Love is not a feeling or an emotion. God's love is constant and is not based on whether we deserve it. His love is without respect of person and is willing to lay down His life for those who are not pure in their love.

*Above all, keep fervent in your love for one another, because **love covers a multitude of sins*** (1 Peter 4:8).

The word *fervent* here means without ceasing.[1] We are to love with that kind of intensity. Mediocrity, the enemy of excellence, is given an open door to enter when we do not love fervently. I think mediocrity can be a curse that is caught like the proverbial flu from another family member. Relationships require work and time, and the neglect of said relationships will slowly erode them until one wonders what went wrong.

A marriage is the perfect picture of how Jesus cares for His Bride the Church. The New Testament covenant is lived out through this mystery of love. What makes this mystery work is that someone is willing to die to his or her own will of selfishness. Marriage is the most unselfish act we will ever do. It requires thought and deliberate actions and being more conscious of the needs and welfare of the one you love than your own.

*Husbands, love your wives, just as Christ loved the church and gave Himself up for her; so that He might sanctify her, having **cleansed her with the washing of water with the word*** (Ephesians 5:25-26).

It is important to note how Jesus cleanses His Bride. He does so by washing her with His Word. The power of His words washes away the effects of all others. When a spouse is wounded by a coworker or perhaps a friend, there is nothing more potent than the words of blessing that come from a husband or wife. A husband who blesses his wife strengthens the cords of the marriage covenant. The power of blessing is the power of love. God so loved that He gave His Son to bless the Church. *Men, we have the kind of wife we bless or we have the kind of wife we curse.*

This phrase came out so clearly in an encounter I had with a man in Houston. It was right after the service and I was in a hurry to get on the road to my next engagement. The pastor of the church, John Parks, requested I talk to a man who was upset. I said I didn't have much time, but I would give a few minutes.

Neither of us knew the man, but he began by saying that his wife was at the lawyer's office at that moment filing for a divorce. He explained that he had been working in Iraq as a civilian contractor. He quickly told us how ungrateful she was and how being away for extended periods was the only way he could stay with her. His anger was vindictive, without any obvious brokenness for the situation. He made the usual accusations and blame.

I stopped him and said, "Sir, you are a curser, and your marriage reflects the kind of wife you have been cursing."

He was angry with the statement and told me he had studied various martial arts and could throw me against the wall just by using his mind.

I concluded by saying, "I must get on the road, but here are some CDs that will help." I gave him the series on the power of blessing and left.

I had the opportunity to be in Houston the next month, and to my surprise, this same man came up to me and said, "Do you remember me?"

I thought to myself, *Yes, I do. This is the guy who wanted to throw me against the wall with his mind.* I acknowledged that I did remember him. This time he had a smile on his face, and his demeanor was noticeably different. Again, my first thought was, *He has found someone else.*

He motioned for a lady to come over to where we were standing. He placed his arm around her and said, "This is my wife of 28 years."

I asked, "What has happened since I saw you last?"

He said, "I reluctantly listened to the teaching on blessing. When my wife came home from the law office, I met her in the hallway and I blessed her using some of the language suggested in the teaching."

His wife described what it was like. She said, "It was strange, because it was as if the words were tangible and moving in slow motion when they hit my heart." She explained the feeling was like liquid love flowing through her body.

They both agreed the last month was like the honeymoon they never had. They now understand the power of blessing that can turn a potential divorce into a covenant of love. Jesus said, *"It is the Spirit who gives life; the flesh profits nothing; the words that I have spoken to you are spirit and are life"* (John 6:63). The cleansing words of blessing can change a heart set on destruction to restoration.

Love does not expose the vulnerability and weaknesses of others. Marriages today show evidence of the enemy's work of division in the home through subtle cursing cloaked in humor or sarcasm. I have listened to husbands and wives at various social gatherings use sarcasm to ridicule their spouse's cooking or their looks just to get a laugh at the expense of their spouse. I understand everyone has their own dynamic in their family and this kind of humor may be understood and accepted. What I am referring to is the kind that tears down through uncovering a weakness in another. It probably did not occur to them they were cursing their own flesh. A man's union with his wife is a covenant agreement that must be upheld and protected. We can do this through blessing her with the washing of words that bring life to her heart.

> *You husbands in the same way, live with your wives in an understanding way, as with someone weaker, since she is a woman; and show her honor as a fellow heir of the grace of life, so **that your prayers will not be hindered*** (1 Peter 3:7).

The word "hinder" in this passage is *ekkopto,* meaning "to frustrate or to cut down."[2] The idea is one who keeps chopping down a tree that he expects fruit to come from. If we want the fruit of love, joy, and peace to come from the marriage, we have to stop chopping at the tree. In the same sense, praying is frustrated when husbands are tearing down their wife while believing for their prayer to be answered.

Submission is not a problem when a husband is blessing his wife as Christ would His Bride, the Church. Submission means to come under the mission. Men, we need to know what the mission is so our wives can come under the mission. The mission is simple—to love the Lord God with all our heart, mind, and strength, and to show forth His goodness through marriage. What woman would have trouble living under that banner of love?

I grew up in a family where exposing one's wife was an art form. Family reunions were occasions for the men to become experts at who could put down their wife using sarcasm. When my wife, Diane, came into the family, she pointed out to me that this is not fun, but instead is uncovering the women in the family and tearing down the trust that a wife has for her husband. She proceeded to explain the security that a wife needs—not just the physical protection but the emotional protection of her husband. I mentioned this to the rest of my family and the cursing ceased due to no one feeding it anymore.

Husbands who endanger their wives with threats of abandoning them or who use money as tactical blackmail need to understand the curse that can come on them for the emotional abuse. I know some of you may be thinking that this is all on the backs of the men. Concerning marriage, the Bible speaks two thirds more to men than women in the New Testament.

When there is an environment of blessing in the home, the children, too, will be at peace and will follow suit in honoring their mother and father. Children can set up their future by learning to bless their parents. The Bible exhorts children to honor their mother and father so that it will go well with them and they will live long on the earth. This is the first commandment with promise.

One of the best cards I ever received came from my son Kevin. He wrote, "Thank you for being a mentor and a friend. Thank you for being a rock that is unmovable for me. You still hold true to what you believe without wavering throughout the years."

Those words meant the world to me. I want my children to know that I have not wavered from the first day that I said, "I love Jesus." The words of blessing coming from your children can enlarge your heart and capacity to love like nothing else will. Love is not just a good idea; it is required when ministering the gifts of the Spirit.

> *Pursue love, yet desire earnestly spiritual gifts, but especially that you may prophesy* (1 Corinthians 14:1).

The apostle Paul makes a *distinction between pursuing and desiring.* In pursuing love, there is effort involved. It implies there is some premeditated thought and planning involved. Desire, by contrast, is a willingness that is hidden and waiting for opportunity. Pursuit implies that opportunity is provided as the action of love becomes a step of faith. Blessing, like love, is a choice of pursuit that is planned for, and then the desire catches up with the pursuit. Pursuing love is simply pursuing the things that reveal the character of the Lord in the relationship. The Bible teaches us that love covers a multitude of sins. Love truly seeks to cover the faults of others.

Years ago, I worked with a guy who delighted in telling the boss the mistakes of the other employees. He was known as a tattletale. He would tell on who was clocking out too early and any other infraction he deemed fuel to further his aspirations. One day, he made a mistake on a project and none of the other employees said a word. Instead, they covered for it and corrected his mistake. Somehow, the boss found out about it, and as a result he lost his job. His error was minor and was not a cause for him to be terminated. However, by exposing the faults of others, he, too, was judged with the same standard he had set. Because he showed no mercy, he was not given any mercy when he needed it.

This principle of covering through blessing was played out with my youngest daughter, Kara. She was preparing for the first week of college when there was a growing confusion in the school's office over her student loan. Somehow, the financial aid department at the school had not filed the appropriate paperwork. Kara consistently attempted to communicate with the clerk about her situation. They appeared not to be interested in solving the problem. She was ready to start school, and the student loans were not coming through. Clearly, the confusion was no fault of Kara's, and the blame began to fly. With time running out, we joined Kara in blessing those in the office who had the authority to correct the problem. Before the week was out, their demeanor had changed and they were very helpful and apologetic. Later, when she went back, they had discovered the error and the whole thing was smoothed over and became retroactive immediately. She had the funding for school just in time.

If we will not be reactive to bad news and will instead be proactive with blessing, things can quickly turn around in our favor. Bless with the awareness that your words are powerful. Life and death are in the tongue. Actually, they begin in the heart, and out of the abundance of the heart they are sown. Backhanded compliments, no matter how cleverly they are disguised, are still deadly. Those who came by at the end of the fiasco funeral and took time to voice their appreciation snatched defeat out of my heart and gave me hope to try it again in the future. I no longer felt like a complete failure to the point of wanting to resign pastoring. Their words of blessing were life to me. What could have been a point of defeat became a point of reference. Since that time I have done countless funeral services of all types, but the turning point was the blessing I received that day. Knowing that what we speak takes on a spiritual life should be enough to make us choose to bless.

> *And He led them out as far as Bethany, and **He lifted up His hands and blessed them**. While He was blessing them, He parted from them and was carried up into Heaven* (Luke 24:50-51).

Those were Jesus' final moments on the earth. Hands lifted up, He blessed the disciples. This was the Aaronic or priestly way of blessing. It is interesting to note Jesus' last act on earth before He ascended was to bless. What a way to go, to end one's ministry with blessing. I try to end each time of ministry with a blessing over those who have been listening to the Word. Sealing the teaching with a blessing is the finale.

PRAYER

Father, I thank You for what You are doing and saying to us in these last days. We want to be a covering church, a covering mother and father. We want to be fathers who know how to love our children. We want to be husbands who understand how to cover our wives. Lord, any areas where we have not been faithful in covering others we ask You to forgive us now. We know that Your Word declares that a child who does not honor their parents cuts their life short. We understand and recognize that when we rightly discern the Lord's Body we will have health and long life (see 1 Cor. 11:29-30). Lord, bring to mind areas we need to cover in blessing. We pray that we would have a new standard in our lives. The standard that we are going to wave is, "I bless you in the name of the Lord, and I bless you coming in, and I bless you going out." We pray that our children and grandchildren will carry blessing, and they will have the favor of the Lord from teachers, bosses, and dignitaries.

Lord, we pray that You would survey our lives and see if there are areas where we have not had the favor of God. Show us areas where we have sabotaged favor through cursing.

Father, we come under Your covering just as Ruth positioned herself at the feet of her redeemer, and he stretched out his mantle and covered her. Thank You for the covering of the Lord Jesus, for when the enemy sees the blood, it has to pass over us. You cover our homes and lives for which we are grateful.

We pray, Lord, that words of life and spirit will flow out of husbands toward their wives. Anoint us, Holy Spirit, to speak over one another with words that are creative.

ENDNOTES

1. Biblesoft's New Exhaustive Strong's Numbers and Concordance with Expanded Greek-Hebrew Dictionary. CD-ROM. Biblesoft, Inc. and International Bible Translators, Inc. (1618).

2. Strong's, *ekkopto* (1581).

Appendix

Blessing Samples

For Any Individual

I bless you in the name of the Lord. I speak over you the purposes of the Kingdom of God to come into your family and life. I speak the peace of God over your family and release you into God's favor and His best. I release upon you the payday and restitution of God coming to you. Whatever the enemy stole from you, let it be returned to you in a greater dimension than the way it left. I bless your children, that they will walk before the Lord and in the fear of Him. May your children rise up and call you blessed. I bless your hands, that as they touch the hands of other people, blessings will come out of them and your mouth.

BLESSING FOR MARRIAGES
(FOR THE MAN AND HIS WIFE TO SPEAK TO EACH OTHER)

I believe that you are a gift from God, and I receive you as my covenant partner. I bless you with the joy of the Lord. I bless you with the peace of God to rule in your heart. May you fulfill all that God has in store for you! Today I bless you as my own flesh, and all the days of your life we will be blessed of the Lord. I am honored to be married to you.

BLESSING TO SPEAK OVER ANYONE

May the eyes of your understanding be opened, and may you come into the full hope of the calling of the Lord (see Eph. 1:17). I bless you with good days and long life. May the favor of the Lord be upon you to live in the fullness of His grace! May I be a blessing to you and may I be able to receive blessing from you.

FOR THE LOCAL CHURCH

Lord, we bless this household of faith. We thank You for the power to bless. We choose to be on the mountain of blessing and declare the blessing of the Lord over Your church. We thank You this church, for its place in the community. We bless this city and may we be a light here. Whatever we do, let us express the love of Christ. Let the power of blessing come through our mouths this week, on the job, in our families, and with our friends. Let our hands be instruments of blessing and our mouth be life. We thank You for the gift of God You have given us to bless and break the curse.

For the Local Church or Family

I bless this house today. I call you fellows and joint heirs of the Kingdom of God. I call you into living the fullness of the Lord. I call you to walk in the freedom of the Spirit wherever the Holy Spirit takes you. You are redeemed from the curse of the law but also redeemed for great purposes in God.

For Families

I bless you with the revelation of Christ and break off any generational repetitive cycles of sabotage. May you come to recognizing the potential of creativity God has placed in you. You have been translated out of the kingdom of darkness into the family of God. Let the power through the blood of Christ free you from every family curse and root that was not planted in you by your heavenly Father. I declare the name of the Son of God over your life. May you fulfill the destiny and purpose of God! May you honor your father and mother and glorify God here on earth. Your Father in Heaven speaks blessings over you. You are His sons and daughters and you have a hope and a future. Your destiny is sealed through the blood of Jesus and your redemption is paid in full. Your inheritance is in store for you, and none will take you from His hand. Live as one blessing what God has blessed, and you will come into the inheritance of your Father in Heaven.

For Favor

I bless you with the influence of the Spirit of Christ. I declare over you that your ceiling will soon be your floor. Those who see you will know the Lord inhabits you with favor. I bless you with relationships that build you up and do not tear you down. May you be able to see farther into your destiny than ever before! I bless you with the peace of God to control every thought and the fear of God to establish your feet.

HEALING FROM EMOTIONAL ABUSE

This is for those who know what it means to be called everything but a child of God. You have pictures framed in your mind and labels pressed upon you that the Holy Spirit wants to tear off your heart. He wants to pull them off like sticky notes and write His name there. Emotional abuse will cause scars on your heart so you are hesitant to trust and be involved with others. God wants to release you from this hindrance.

You might be the one that is the abuser and have used accusations and despairing words to wound. The Lord will heal your memory of what has taken place as you read the prayer.

EMOTIONAL HEALING PRAYER

Jesus, we appeal to you as the Bridegroom. Come as a loving Husband and show us what it means to bless and not curse. You have proven You love us so much because You laid down Your life. Come and minister healing to every wife, husband, or young person that has been abused by verbal barrage. Heal the hearts where there are gaping wounds of the past. I release the healing virtue of the Lord to enter the place of the wounding. May your sleep be restful without fear of night terror. Amen.

You May Contact
Pastor Kerry Kirkwood by:

E-mail: kerry@trinityfellowship.com
Web site: www.trinityfellowship.com